Navigating the NHS
core issues for clinicians

Edited by

PETER LEES

Senior Lecturer in Neurosurgery
Director of Research and Development
Southampton University Hospitals NHS Trust

Foreword by

Sir Kenneth Calman

Chief Medical Officer
Department of Health

THE BRITISH ASSOCIATION
OF MEDICAL MANAGERS

Radcliffe Medical Press
Oxford and New York

© 1996 Peter Lees

Radcliffe Medical Press Ltd
18 Marcham Road, Abingdon, Oxon OX14 1AA, UK

Radcliffe Medical Press, Inc.
141 Fifth Avenue, New York, NY 10010, USA

British Library Cataloguing in Publication Data

A catalogue record for this book is available from the British Library.

ISBN 1 85775 106 X

Library of Congress Cataloging-in-Publication Data

Navigating the NHS: core issues for clinicians/edited by Peter Lees;
  foreword by Kenneth Calman.
    p. cm.
  Includes bibliographical references and index.
  ISBN 1–85775–106–X
  1. National Health Service (Great Britain).   2. Health care reform – Great Britain
  I. Lees, Peter.
  [DNLM: 1. National Health Service (Great Britain).   2. State Medicine – organization &
  administration – Great Britain.   3. Health Care Reform – history – Great Britain.
  W 225 FA1 N3 1996]
  RA395.G6N376   1996
  362.1'0941–dc20
  DNLM/DLC
  for Library of Congress   96-13731
                                                                                       CIP

Typeset by Marksbury Multimedia Ltd, Midsomer Norton, Avon.
Printed in Great Britain by BPC Wheatons Ltd, Exeter

Contents

List of contributors

Peter Beck, *Medical Director, Rotherham District General Hospital, Moorgate Road, Oakwood, Rotherham, South Yorkshire S60 2UD*

Andrew Boon, *Consultant Pathologist, Department of Cytopathology, St James' University Hospital, Leeds LS9 7TF*

Murray Cochrane, *Director of Developments, Cornwall and the Isles of Scilly Health Authority, John Keay House, St Austell, Cornwall PL25 4NQ*

Celia Cramp, *Clinical Director, St Helens and Knowsley Hospitals, Whiston Hospital, Warrington Road, Prescot, Merseyside L35 5DR*

Steve George, *Lecturer in Public Health Medicine, Southampton University Hospitals NHS Trust, Tremona Road, Southampton, Hants SO16 6YD*

Peter Grime, *Senior Registrar in Oral and Maxillo-facial Surgery, Southampton University Hospitals NHS Trust, Tremona Road, Southampton, Hants SO16 6YD*

Stephen Holgate, MRC *Clinical Professor of Immunopharmacology, Southampton University Hospitals NHS Trust, Tremona Road, Southampton, Hants SO16 6YD*

Peter Lees, *Senior Lecturer, Honorary Consultant Neurosurgeon and Director of Research and Development, Wessex Neurological Centre, Southampton University Hospitals NHS Trust, Tremona Road, Southampton, Hants SO16 6YD*

Tony Lockett, *Associate Director, Corning Besselaar Ltd, 7 Roxborough Way, Maidenhead, Berks SL6 3UD*

Sue Lydeard, *Quality Development Manager, Southampton University Hospitals NHS Trust, Tremona Road, Southampton, Hants SO16 6YD*

John Richards, *Head of Performance and Development, Southampton and South West Hampshire Health Authority, Oakley Road, Southampton, Hants SO9 4WQ*

Tim Scott, *Senior Fellow, BAMM, Barnes Hospital, Kingsway, Cheadle, Cheshire SK8 2NY*

TONY SHAW, *Chief Executive, Southampton and South West Hampshire Health Authority, Oakley Road, Southampton, Hants SO16 4GX*

JENNY SIMPSON, *Chief Executive, BAMM, Barnes Hospital, Kingsway, Cheadle, Cheshire SK8 2NY*

PAUL STAFFORD, *Director, Secta Management Consulting, Shelley Farm, Shelley Lane, Ower, Hants SO51 6AS*

BOB YOUNG, *Consultant Physician, Department of Endocrinology, Salford Royal Hospitals NHS Trust, Hope Hospital, Stott Lane, Salford M6 8HD*

Foreword

The title of this book intrigued me. It conjured up nautical images of charts, maps, shoals, rocks, wind, rain and storms. It suggested instruments to determine course and direction, compass and sextant. And of course it is a good metaphor. Understanding the NHS is about knowing where you are going and how to get there. The image of the course of a large tanker being changed by many tugs also came to mind. The NHS does need to change, but it will only do so if there are a number of willing and powerful forces at work.

But the image also begs several questions. The first and most obvious, is what is the destination? This is a key question, and the answer to it sets the tone for the chapters in the book. Is it about financial issues? Is it about career progression for staff? Is it about managing the workforce? For me the answer relates to the primary purpose of the NHS which is to meet the needs of patients and the population, and to put them first. It means involving patients and the public more in determining what is required and how best it can be achieved. It is first and foremost about values. This is of course simplistic and such an objective has within it a series of contraindications and conflicts. But at least it gives a sense of purpose and direction to the organization.

But what do we need to get there? Again to stretch the nautical example, there is a need for good management, teamwork and leadership. Without these the ship will not function effectively and mutiny may even occur! Working together in partnership is crucial, as is the recognition of the skills and expertise of all members of the crew. In particular the captain needs to earn respect and ensure that all members of the team are pulling in the same direction.

Then, there is the issue of instruments available to chart the course, monitor performance, measure the distance travelled and identify problems ahead. The radar function is important (intelligence) as is the need to continually improve the methods available to control the direction (research). In addition the members of the crew need to be regularly updated on these matters (education) and be helped to do so.

This book sets out to chart some of these issues. It provides practical solutions to problems, and gives examples for others to take up or reject.

Finally, it is perhaps important to stress that navigation and nautical manoeuvres are not always easy. In doing so, particularly when the environment is changing rapidly, the quality of life of the crew also needs to be considered. The staff are our most important asset, we need to think of them too. This book also gives some insights into how that might be done.

Sir Kenneth Calman
March 1996

Preface

In just over a decade the NHS has undergone the most widespread changes since its inception. Such has been the pace of change that unless you were at the heart of the 'reforms' in the early 1980s you would be forgiven for wondering where we came from and probably why. If proof of that confusion were needed it can be found regularly among my senior registrar colleagues when applying for consultant posts. Those clinicians perceived to have a leaning towards 'medical management' seldom enjoy much interest until that fateful time and will be very familiar with the oft-posed request, 'tell me something about management, I have an interview tomorrow'.

The stimulus for this book was to help medical trainees understand the huge health care management 'industry' which has developed so rapidly and which nowadays impacts upon us all, but such is the calibre of my co-authors' contributions that this book has relevance to anyone trying to negotiate their way around 'today's NHS'.

Using the history of the reforms as a backdrop, we have chosen discrete topics (presented in broadly logical order) representing the major new initiatives, with a bias towards the secondary care sector. The authors were asked to make their chapters stand-alone, accessible for the uninitiated and to imagine they were on the train en route to 'the interview' and had the sudden urge to 'mug-up' on a pertinent topic quickly.

I conclude with an invitation. With the current pace of change, further editions of this book are anticipated and ideas for inclusion next time would be warmly welcomed.

Peter Lees
March 1996

Acknowledgements

This was not a solo effort and I am grateful for help and encouragement from a number of people. All the authors are busy professionals but still kept perfectly to deadlines. Sir Kenneth Calman, the Chief Medical Officer, has kindly written the Foreword and Dr Jenny Simpson and Tim Scott (of the British Association of Medical Managers (BAMM)) have not only contributed directly but have also given inestimable advice on the subject areas and whom to approach as contributors. Peter Grime and Tim Lees, trainees at the time, gave invaluable comment upon whether the objectives of the book were being met. Gillian Nineham and her colleagues at Radcliffe Medical Press have taught me a lot and with great patience. The speed that Radcliffe turn such a tome into the printed book has impressed me enormously. Those of you who, like me, are fortunate enough to work with an outstanding secretary will appreciate the huge contribution of my personal assistant, Clair Wilkinson.

To Doris and our daughter, Hannah, who was born during the final preparation of the book

1 Introduction

Peter Grime

On the road to Damascus

Several years ago I made a decision to pursue a career in hospital medicine, not as a physician (affectionately referred to in our unit as the 'clever doctors') but as a simple surgeon. I made a list, as is my custom when I have a decision to make: 'the advantages and disadvantages of achieving consultant status'. I did not, indeed could not, at that time list any disadvantages, but my list of advantages was long and positive: a consultant post was for life, I would be my own boss, run my own department and be free to run things as I decided. The financial rewards would be excellent: good salary, good fringe benefits and good private practice potential. Although it was going to take some considerable time with a lot of hard work to get where I wanted to go, I have never been afraid of hard work and knew that I had the talent to succeed. I could expect that, when I achieved consultant status, my work intensity would decrease and the hours of 'hands -on' work would diminish. There would be enough junior staff to do the necessary routine work and that would free me to concentrate on 'higher things'. The amount of 'boring' clinical work would go down, and I would be free to choose the service that I provided. I viewed management in simple terms. Hospital administrators (managers) would be there to facilitate the success of my department and minimize any inconvenience to both myself and my staff. I would make the decisions (manage) but have little to do with the day-to-day implementation (administration).

A classical hospital medical or surgical training reinforces the belief that you are correct, that you know best. This 'apprenticeship' is long and hard and produces like-minded survivors: egotistical, arrogant, single minded, determined, to name but a few of the 'surgical' personality traits that one requires to succeed. One had, and still has, to be careful of the 'old boy' network, which has great power to ensure either a smooth progression through the 'ranks' of the 'King's Own Scalpels' or a rapid demobilization! The ability to perform surgery and manage patients should be an advantage, but one's main duty is to toe the party line, kiss the occasional frog, never get romantically entangled with a consultant's daughter or wife and never, ever do anything to interfere with the smooth running of the boss's private practice! Taking all things into consideration, I could smell the sweetness of success.

Unfortunately things did not go quite the way I wanted them to. I managed to fall foul of 'the system'. For some inexplicable reason I began to think independently or to be more honest. I began to speak and act more independently and committed a heinous crime. I suffered 'opinions', probably borne out of a frustrated development, and deviated from the accepted path of behaviour. When the time came to move from registrar to senior registrar, interviews came and went, and subsequently dried up! I was facing a crisis in my personal and professional life. As a consequence I did what I always do when difficult decisions have to be made; I reverted to self-analysis and made my lists again. Analyse, conclude, act! What is wrong with me? Why does nobody want me? I am good at my job, enthusiastic, hard working, innovative; my curriculum vitae is excellent. How could anybody not want me? The list contained personal good points, perceived bad points, points for going on, points for career change. Do I really want to be a consultant now? I revised my list of the advantages and disadvantages of achieving consultant status in the health service. On this occasion I could not list any advantages, yet the list of disadvantages was long and of consider-able concern.

By this time the White Paper[1] had arrived and the 'new-style' National Health Service (NHS) management was born: proactive rather than reactive (to the medical profession) management; passive administration; rolling contracts with poor job security and a decreasing salary in real terms (perhaps under the guise of performance-related pay); an increasing work intensity because of an emphasis on work-load targets; the decreasing number of junior staff with their limited hours 'on call' and fewer consultants (probably redesignated more simply as 'specialists') than would be needed to fill 'the gaps'; less clinical freedom and more market-oriented practice; income generation; internal markets; management growth with an unwelcome 'interference' in clinical matters; audit and information technology (number crunching *par excellence*); the Patient's Charter; low staff morale; attacks on private practice and associated media hype implying poor consultant performance; a decrease in status, with consultants perceived as 'just another employee – easily replaced!'

I began to view management in a different light, something that had been taken away from, and turned against, the profession. The worm had turned! The oppressed administrator, sick to death of arrogant, self-opinionated doctors, grasped the opportunity to strike back under the guise of 'NHS reform'.

It appeared that my potential job, if indeed there was to be one, was not worth bothering about, an understandable attitude given rationalization of thought for self-preservation.

Unfortunately I had reached the stage at which a career change was impractical: not at my age and with a young family to support. I had to go on and make the best of it! After a number of interviews, when I really felt that the end was nigh and I was about to sink without trace, I finally convinced an appointments committee to give me a chance and (gratefully) got on with it. Once in the lifeboat I did not want to reach the point of applying for consultant posts before revising my attitude, giving serious thought to future practice and the role of a consultant in the 'new NHS'; after all I still needed to reach dry land.

Looking back I could see two superficially different, yet deeply similar, unproductive approaches to the consultant role (in both clinical practice and management). My first deliberations were positive and rather self-focused. I suspect, but cannot be sure, that I assumed an intention to play my part in the NHS to the best of my ability. Surgical practice in the NHS would be clinically and financially rewarding to me. I saw myself in a dominant, quasi-managerial role, in control, making decisions for implementation by someone else. My revised, later, list was extremely negative, although still self-focused, and my attitude to the perceived loss of management control was reactive, a somewhat paranoid view ('It is not fair, they are out to get me. Resist all change, do not co-operate'), a view devoid of rational thought for a supposedly intelligent, well-educated professional. 'What do they know about health care and managing patients? I know best, and I should be making the decisions'.

The NHS had changed for the worse because I was not going to get an awful lot out of it! To be frank I am now appalled, as I hope you the reader are appalled, at this negative behaviour. I have never considered myself to be a negative person. I had not even recognized, until it was pointed out to me, that both lists were devoid of one important sentiment. Not once had I ever mentioned the 'patient' (the customer). I appeared to see everything in terms of me and what I wanted and never in terms of what the patient needed or wanted. What was I going to get out of it? I could see myself as part of the problem rather than the solution.

Clinical education and training teaches us to listen, observe, examine, investigate, conclude, act, review and change opinion if necessary. If we are honest, the provision of health care in this country has been haphazard and sometimes illogical, too often based on personal opinion rather than proven value. The management of acute and emergency problems has generally been first class, unlike the care in chronic disease, the management of which is all too often less than desirable. Changes in management have to be both clinical and administrative if we are to get the best value from available resources.

I needed, indeed wanted, to review my attitude to health care and my role in the provision of services. What would I do if I were managing (running) my own business? How would I go about providing health care? I sat down and produced the following list of questions: What do my patients (customers) want? What do they need? Do I want to increase the range of services I provide? Am I in a position to change and respond quickly, as required? Can I provide the goods now? Do I have the appropriate skills? Do I have the ability to develop skills, and even if I do, do I actually want or need to develop them? Do I need to buy in skills? What facilities do I need? What facilities do I have at the moment, and do I want or need to develop those facilities accordingly? Can I afford to do that, and if I go ahead, will I be able to meet the needs and the demands that those extra facilities will generate? Can I increase my income without incurring extra costs (in other words can I reduce unit cost and liberate income?) Could I generate income from loans, get enough business to repay them and still provide myself with enough personal income? Would I actually get more customers if I made these changes, and where would they come from? What is the competition doing that I am not? What could I provide that the competition is not? Whether or not they need it, would my customers actually want it? What would I charge? Would it be enough to cover my expenses, or would I price myself out of the market? Do we have adequate representatives in the 'field', and are we reaching all our potential customers?

Encouraged by my efforts I made another list of questions, assuming I would be running the business for someone else: What do our customers want and need now? What will our customers want and need in the future? Is our organization geared up to providing those wants and needs at a competitive price and acceptable quality? If it is not, what do we need to do to correct the situation? Do we need more staff? Can we get better facilities? Become more efficient? What can we do to help the business to succeed?

In order to make decisions (manage), I would need information. I could not make decisions, nor answer the inevitable questions posed by customers, without the relevant facts and figures. The customers would be expected to enquire about 'results' and I would expect to produce evidence of my ability to provide a 'quality' service. (Customers expect a reasonable service at a competitive cost.) I would need to provide my customers with the goods they wanted and to deal with them in a quiet and efficient manner, responding to their comments and criticisms. The business would operate to a set of reasonable standards, of which my customers would be made aware. That, after all, is the business way.

What became very evident to me was that this 'business approach' differs from the archetypal 'medical management' typified by the character of Sir Lancelot Spratt in the 'Doctor' series by Richard Gordon and by my own early aspirations. The traditional medical approach is almost exclusively self-focused: 'I know best, you get what I provide and like it! I am the most important person and deserve the biggest income'. The business way is predominantly customer-focused, given that the questions asked should lead to the provision of a service that the customer needs or wants rather than that which the doctor wishes to provide. Salaries paid to all employees reflect availability and maintenance of the work-force: employers will only pay what is needed to keep staff and get the job done (without dropping to unacceptable standards).

Looking at the questions posed I recognized an all too familiar scenario – aspects of the NHS reforms – not in 'management' jargon but in 'plain speak'. I recognised *audit* (what are we doing, how are we doing?); *research and development* (what should we be doing, how do we improve on the present?); *marketing* (what does the customer want?) or *customer focusing* (providing for the needs of the customer); *information technology* (computer-oriented gathering of vital facts and figures); *quality control* (service to a satisfactory standard); *resource management* (getting the best out of staff, equipment and facilities and keeping the costs down) or *value from resources*; *efficiency gains* (reducing unit costs to release capital); *contracting* (guarantees of work and control, therefore of income and, to some extent, expenditure); *The Patient's Charter* (working to a set of reasonable, published standards of business practice and a declaration of intent to provide a satisfactory service).

Ask yourself the question, how would you run a business with an annual turnover exceeding £70 million (the annual budget of an 'average' NHS Trust)? It makes good business sense to budget for income and expenditure, to cut the cloth according to the purse. Devolving budgets to individual units, departments or directorates encourages self-reliance and promotes inventiveness, providing that the degree of central control remains unobtrusive. Changes in practice can lead to efficiency gains and liberation of finances to spend on better, or more extensive, services. Without the ability to generate true income, however (the 'pot' is a fixed size), there must be a limit to what can be achieved. With 'winners' there will always be 'losers'; one directorate may grow as another contracts, one area may benefit as another suffers. To that end not all the NHS reforms are desirable, and I do not suggest that the medical profession embraces any philosophy without question. We are one of the key guardians of patient welfare and must remain so. It is our responsibility, however, to ensure the provision of the best service possible from given resources and that can only be achieved by working within the system, by placing ourselves in a position to influence policy in the widest sense. It is difficult for a reasonable person not to respond to a well-reasoned argument. The medical profession has been handed a golden opportunity, through the reforms, to influence health care in a manner not previously possible. The reforms will not go away and neither should we assume that further reform will not take place.

Perhaps the medical profession has already failed the NHS, just as consultants of the past have failed those of the future by burying their heads in the sand and hoping it will all go away, by bleating about change that any sensible profession should have instituted long ago under proper self-regulation, and by failing to grasp the initiative, relinquishing a managerial role to non-medical personnel.

I am thankful that my early misfortune to be cursed with a 'bad attitude' has opened my eyes and my ears and closed my mouth to ill-conceived words. I wish that my change in attitude had come about through maturity and wisdom rather than the threat of unemployment, yet I believe with a passion felt only by the converted. The health service has the potential to be better than it has ever been. The foundations are being laid for the future with the birth of evidence-based medical practice.

Change inevitably has its price, and perhaps it should not be unexpected that those who lived with the old system cannot live with the new. For those prepared to be involved, to co-operate (doctors can and will make good managers) a fulfilling career will be realized. I implore you, the reader, to pursue a similar exercise to my own, to read and digest the contents of this book. We, as a profession, need good managers and all of us should have a working knowledge of how to manage. Join us!

Reference

1   Department of Health (1989) *Working for Patients* (Cmnd 555). HMSO, London.

2 Where are we now? The NHS in the mid-1990s

Tim Scott

Trying to describe the current NHS is not a leisurely activity to be undertaken on a Sunday afternoon. This is no quiet country meadow, where one can set up easel, mix paints and depict a harmonious, tranquil setting. People working in the NHS feel their situation to be much more akin to white water rafting the Colorado river. Any thought of describing a particular bend in the river, with its treacherous swirls and eddies, is lost in the need to try to spot the shoals under the water ahead and keep the raft from hitting the side walls of the canyon.

To talk about a high degree of change in the NHS is to dilute the reality with management jargon; there are few givens, the language changes as fast as the structural framework, and no-one, least of all government, has a clear understanding of where it will all take us.

Even to attempt to discuss the so-called NHS reforms introduced by the White Paper *Working for Patients* (1989)[1] is to suggest that there was somehow a steady-state NHS before the reforms and a modified NHS some time afterwards. The reforms were in fact a further major and radical reshaping of an NHS already subject to a variety of change factors.

NHS management from 1983

Where then should we start the story? In 1974 with the area health authorities? In 1982 with the abolition of those area health authorities? Each intervention has added its own momentum and created its own language. One starting point might be the famous Griffiths NHS management enquiry. On 6 October 1983, the late Sir Roy Griffiths reported in a letter to the Secretary of State on the review of NHS management that he had been asked to undertake in February of that year. He pointed out that 'surprisingly, given the welter of the reports on almost every aspect of the NHS over the past thirty years, there has been no major review of the internal management of the hospitals since the Bradber report of 1954'. He then proceeded with a series of recommendations on how the whole thing should be actively managed rather than passively administered. In this report, which was seized on and implemented by government, we see many of the seeds of the subsequent reforms.[2] In particular the introduction of general management was the most visible aspect of Griffiths' desire to see a more business-like environment permeating the NHS.

One of Griffiths' recommendations was the creation of the NHS Advisory Board (subsequently reshaped as the NHS Policy Board). This structure, drawing on an industrial model, provided a range of advice to the Secretary of State, drawn not only from the civil service, as was customary, but also from a variety of major industrialists. One of the significant advantages has been that Sir Roy himself, and a number of others, provided a continuity across the inevitable Cabinet reshuffles over the past decade.

During the 1980s the developing implications of the Griffiths' prescription were unfolding in the NHS. For example, Griffiths had wished to see the rapid introduction of much more sophisticated budgeting and control systems. Initial experiments, under the title of 'management budgeting', ran aground as in a number of places they exposed the cultural and value system differences between doctors and administrative staff, principally finance professionals. In 1986 a modified set of initiatives known as resource management, constructed in conjunction with the clinical professionals, sought to develop more appropriate organizational management structures and management information systems, with a particular commitment to the involvement of clinical professionals in such structures.

Another major symptom of the developing business culture of the NHS was the emphasis on contracting out services. The market-based Conservative government, in power since 1979, saw many opportunities in the public sector for competitive tendering for services, and a 1983 programme from the Department of Health (DoH) required health authorities to put forward programmes for domestic cleaning, catering and laundry. Significant financial gains were achieved, and, perhaps more importantly, discussion was opened up on what really needed to be done 'in house' and what could be contracted out. By 1987 the process had begun to spread to other non-clinical services, such as portering, transport and computing, and later it reached support clinical services, including diagnostic and pathology services.

One particular aspect of NHS accounting that came under increasing pressure was a lack of any true accounting for capital or valuing of capital assets, including the estates and land. The need to ensure a 'level playing field' with external organizations in the tendering process, as well as to force more rational decision making in areas including hospital building and equipment purchasing, led to a series of technical financial modifications, which can again be seen as precursors to the 1989 White Paper.

White Paper (1989) reforms

Much anecdotal evidence exists to suggest that the one year review of the NHS to which Mrs Thatcher committed herself in 1988 came as a surprise, not only to the civil service but even to her cabinet colleagues. The late 1980s had seen a succession of funding-based crisis issues, particularly during the winter of 1987/88. The working group took evidence privately and did not consult in any meaningful way. One of the individuals with access to this inner circle of thinking was Professor Enthoven, an American economist who had in 1985 set out a model of how a market might operate in the NHS. Although the working group was ostensibly set up as a reaction to public concern over the overall financing of the NHS, it became clear that this was not in fact a topic for debate, but that government, and Mrs Thatcher in particular, believed that far greater value could be obtained from existing investment.

The reforms, when finally set out, surprised many. This was because there was little detail, either in the main document or the subsidiary working papers. Many of the radical ideas being put forward seemed to be only partially thought through and indeed potentially at odds with one another. In broad measure they could be set out as:

- the creation of a split between those responsible for purchasing health care and those responsible for providing it
- a set of contracts to be negotiated and agreed, specifying health care to be provided at a price and within other contractual terms
- a requirement for all doctors to undertake medical audit
- the creation of self-governing NHS Trusts
- the creation of fundholding general practices.

Purchaser–provider split

The fundamental element of the reforms was the decision to split the NHS into two constituent elements; those whose responsibility was to consider the needs of particular defined populations and determine what services should be provided for that population, and those, in provider organizations, who would undertake the contracts for health care offered by such purchasers. Whilst the White Paper made explicit the mechanism by which purchasers were to be separated from providers and set out the organizational structure (much comment focused on these practicalities), the underlying concept was in itself a very powerful clarification of the sometimes conflicting and ambiguous roles that had in the past been undertaken by the statutory organizations. Many district health authorities (DHAs) had struggled to find ways to invest more in community-based services, whilst their hospitals represented the single largest employer in the locality.

Hospitals themselves had been caught in the 'efficiency trap'. Treating ever-increasing numbers of patients, even at significantly reduced costs, meant that individual hospitals required additional funding. Under the complex funding arrangements, which differed from region to region, such increases in 'cross-boundary flows' might only affect monies received at best some two years later. Hospitals that attempted to tackle growing waiting lists by increasing their efficiency suffered from this funding gap. One of the avowed intentions of the reforms was that 'money should follow patients', i.e. if patient flows to individual organizations increased, so should their funding. The logical consequence in a cash-limited health service, which was not made explicit, is that any hospital managing to attract more funds because it attracted more patients can do so only at the expense of other hospitals seen to be 'losing' patients.

The extent to which this free market might be allowed to develop was a key question during the early stages of the reforms. The potentially dramatic impact on London in the end necessitated a major market intervention, the establishment of the London Implementation Group (LIG), and the pace at which hospitals and localities outside the M25 have been able to increase the numbers of patients they treat, and stem the flows into London, has been considerably constrained.

At the outset, it seemed as if many of those involved in management within the NHS, who came originally from a hospital or community background, moved swiftly into organizational positions within the new provider units. To balance this, efforts of the DoH were to some extent concentrated on developing a strong purchasing function, since little explicit purchasing of health care had previously been undertaken. Throughout the country health authorities merged with each other to become commissioning agents (note the subtle shift in terminology) with responsibility for significant populations. These commissioning agencies have not stabilized; there are at least two factors still shifting their configuration and indeed internal organizations. In the first place the major review, which looked at the functions and structures of the NHS at higher levels, has seen the rethinking on the number and role of regions. Additionally, the need for close working between family health services authorities (FHSAs) and DHAs, reflected in many places by the creation of joint purchasing discussion fora and indeed agencies, will lead to the creation of single organizations responsible for all these functions.

Trusts

Health-providing organizations, hospitals, community units and so on were to be set up as self-governing Trusts. Any particular configuration could put forward a Trust proposal, and, if the Secretary of State considered that they had a reliable future and business plan, would be made a Trust, with a chairman appointed by Secretary of State and a board of trustees. In effect such a Trust would have buildings and equipment on loan from the government and would in return be required to pay interest on the debt. However, apart from providing a return on investment, Trusts were not intended to make profits, and any surplus was to be reinvested. Trusts were set up with potential for a considerable number of 'freedoms', including the ability to negotiate and agree pay and conditions with staff outside the national Whitley council rates. There were undoubtedly inducements to the more well-managed and active units to put themselves forward for Trust status, and the 57 first wave applicants received considerable developmental support from the DoH. The next two years saw increasing pressure on the balance of the units, described as 'directly managed', to shift to Trust status. The re-election of the Conservative government removed any lingering doubts or hopes that the reforms might be reversed, and the inevitability of Trust status became the cultural norm.

More interesting perhaps than the routine numbers of Trusts announced year on year has been the reconfiguration of some. Most spectacularly perhaps, the Guy's Hospital Trust, often described as the flagship of the reforms, has been forced into a shotgun marriage with St Thomas', reflecting the influence that the Tomlinson report[3] and the LIG have had on the capital. Another major constraint on configurations has been the shift away from 'whole district Trusts'. There was a tendency in the early Trust proposals, particularly in some geographical areas such as Manchester and Lancashire, for proposals for hospitals and linked community services to be regarded as a single Trust unit. Whilst a number of these were accepted, there was some reconsideration of the principles, and the DoH began strongly to advise against such proposals unless there were exceptional circumstances. Whilst merger configurations are being considered where there is the possibility of rationalizing sites, the general approach is for single discrete units of management of between £50m and £150m turnover.

Clinical directorates

In accord with its stated intentions of devolution, the NHS Executive (NHSE) has not put forward prescriptive requirements for the internal management structure of Trusts. There are clearly a number of givens: the chairman of the Trust is appointed by the Secretary of State, and the membership of the Trust board is fixed, with an equal number of non-executive and executive directors. These latter include the chief executive, the medical director, the director of finance, the director of nursing and one other as seems locally appropriate. What is left to the Trust's own judgement, however, is how they manage internally. Within hospital Trusts in particular, the preferred model is often referred to as the clinical directorate structure. The detailed features of such structures, which essentially create strong devolved units of management headed up by clinical staff, have been researched and reviewed by a group made up of British Association of Medical Managers (BAMM), British Medical Association (BMA), Institute of Health Service Management (IHSM) and Royal College of Nursing (RCN). They jointly issued a research-based booklet entitled *Managing Clinical Services – a consensus statement of principles for effective clinical management*,[4] based on detailed study of this kind of arrangement in a variety of units. The clinical directorate structures and hospitals in which they have emerged provide links back to the resource management programme. It was the resource management programme and its pilot hospitals that first raised the topic of internal structures, and those hospitals, notably Guy's, publicly discussed and debated the merits of formally involving clinical staff in management. The medical consultants, who in large measure took on the clinical directorate role, often did so at personal expense to both income and career and in unstable and difficult situations. Nevertheless the emerging consensus demonstrates the importance of this particular step.

GP fundholders

The most unexpected element of the 1989 White Paper was the proposal to establish fundholding GP practices. Subsequently described as the chilli powder in the stew of the reforms, fundholding practices were to some extent drawn from and modelled on the health maintenance organizations (HMOs) established in the USA in the 1970s. Practices of a reasonable size, originally 11 000 but subsequently reduced to 9000, were to be allowed to manage funds to pay for a variety of treatments, including elective surgery at local hospitals. The practices, which tended inevitably to be multihanded, had to demonstrate that they had the management and business capacity to take on the responsibility and were then to be given a budget, calculated around their current referral patterns, to cover non-emergency inpatient work in a variety of elective surgical areas, outpatient visits, diagnostic testing and an 'indicative' budget for drugs.

These budgets, which were of the order of £1 million − £2 million for the larger practices, would give the practice the opportunity to use the money for alternative purposes, such as investment in practice premises or employment of additional practice staff, in the event that savings could be made. The intention was clearly to provide an incentive to reduce pressures on hospital services and to provide a clinical quality control on elective surgery. There were, and still are, a number of concerns about the whole principle of fundholding practices, to which the Labour party has declared its opposition. The most significant criticism, is the accusation that they create a two-tier service, i.e. that their contract leverage means that their patients will be treated differently, better or more swiftly by hospitals. The level of concern was such that the DoH was forced in 1990 to issue a circular clearly reiterating the principle that only clinical priority should determine priority for admission for hospital treatment.

Nevertheless the success story of fundholding practices has been that they have negotiated a better quality of service for their clients and in many cases raised standards and expectations, both with the general public and with other GPs. As the criteria have been relaxed to enable more practices to become fundholding, the percentage of the population covered by fundholding practices increased so that, by 1993/94, 25% of the population of England were in fundholding practices. This figure contains quite substantial variation, some regions having a third of their population covered by fundholding practices. Yet, because only certain elements of hospital budgets for non-emergency specified elective operations are included, still only a small percentage of the total hospital and community health budget is being passed through fundholding practices. Even so they constitute a very significant element, and research conducted by the London School of Economics, funded by the King's Fund Institute, has revealed the range of innovation and change that they have stimulated. Quite simply they have changed the nature of the relationship between the hospital consultant and the GP. For many fundholding practices the fundamentals under discussion during contract negotiation were not particularly to do with price or even clinical quality, but about quite simple matters such as the availability of hospital consultants to discuss patients and the daily pick-up and delivery of test results. A number of large hospitals, too busy to discuss what seemed to be relatively trifling matters, were horrified to find that practices had happily switched their allegiance, not merely for pathology tests but also even for particular aspects of surgery. Although the sums involved as a percentage of the hospitals' overall budget were relatively trivial, it is these kinds of marginal change that hospitals find difficult to accommodate, especially in the short-term.

The full potential of fundholding practices, and the extent to which the budget for health services might be managed by the fundholding practices, is still not agreed. Experiments are being undertaken on passing the totality of budget for a local population to a number of practices (total fundholding), but major questions arise both about the role of the health authority as purchaser and about the ability of Secretary of State to influence patterns of health care through independent contractors.

Medical audit

The requirement set out in the White Paper that medical staff be involved in routine and regular audit has had a mixed course. Politically it was seen as a necessary check to counter claims that overall quality would reduce in a market for health, since buyers would go for the cheapest product. The intention was that doctors, through self-regulating mechanisms, would ensure that the quality of clinical work in hospitals was maintained and improved rather than allowed to deteriorate in any way. Considerable sums of money were provided by the DoH, albeit taken from the overall health care budget, to stimulate and develop audit in hospitals. Responses have been very mixed. Whilst some specialties in some hospitals do undertake rigorous audits on a structured and planned basis, they probably comprise a relatively small percentage. In many hospitals the monies have been either used to support research or diluted in other ways. Typically, in many specialties, a monthly meeting reviews a number of cases in a somewhat unstructured way.

The position has been further complicated by subsequent moves by the DoH to promote clinical audit, intended to involve the whole multi-disciplinary team who participate in patient care. This currently sits uneasily in many hospitals alongside medical audit, which is not yet sufficiently mature to involve other disciplines. The other major problem is the lack of linkage between medical or clinical audit and the routine management processes of the hospital. Many hospitals have developed some form of quality control, quality assurance or quality improvement, with a few attempting total quality management (TQM). Audit has in only a few cases been integrated into these broader management initiatives. In the remaining hospitals the result is that management issues often uncovered by audit remain unaddressed and the worlds of organizational management and clinical management are perceived as in some way different from each other.

Contracts

The 1989 White Paper was seen by many to be theoretical and not based on any detailed development work. The government chose to characterize all calls for experimentation and development as attempts to block the process of change, and determined that the principles would be implemented nationwide on 1 April 1991. The management response, from both the NHSE and the regions, was 'steady state' and 'smooth take-off'. In other words the implementation of contracts was not to be seen as an opportunity to reshape health care in any major way at that time, but that contracts should basically reflect current realities. Some regions, for example North Western, took this even further and insisted that contracts should preserve the status quo for three years. Most initial contracts were block contracts, i.e. they agreed an overall sum of money for hospital services to be provided to the same level as previously. Subsequent pressure from the DoH, as well as natural development of the market, has meant a shift towards cost and volume contracts. By this is meant contracts that specify a price per, for example, hospital episode and volume (number of episodes) for the contract as a whole, with quite often contractual specification of acceptable tolerance and thresholds that will trigger changes in payment.

Costing systems, initially primitive and useful only at the level of clinical specialty are being developed, with experimental work looking for a move towards comparing costs from one contract to another for specific groups of patients (health care resource groups (HRGs)). There is an inevitable tension between the centre's desire, on the one hand, to allow a variety of approaches to contracting, with local circumstances dictating the type and nature of the contract, and on the other, to be able to compare contracts from one part of the country with those of another. The argument will always be that what is being purchased in one place is apples and what is being purchased in another is oranges, and the development of a national standard set of groups (HRGs) for patients is an attempt to achieve and agree on acceptable standardization.

Evaluation to date

The government rejected any attempts to set up formal research and evaluation; this was to be the way forward. A publication by the King's Fund Institute, summarizing independently commissioned research, was cautiously optimistic, suggesting that 'there is potential for real gains arising from the reforms'.[5] What no-one would disagree with is that the NHS has been fundamentally reshaped, and whatever organizational structures might be adopted in the future, there is a far clearer understanding of the distinct and different roles of commissioning health care and providing it.

References

1 Department of Health (1989) *Working for Patients* (Cmnd 555). HMSO, London.
2 DHSS (1983) *NHS Management Enquiry* (The Griffiths Report) DA (83)38. DHSS, London.
3 Department of Health (1994) *NHS Services in London* (The Tomlinson Enquiry). DoH, London.
4 IHSM (1993) *Managing Clinical Services*. BAMM (with BMA, IHSM and RCN), London.
5 King's Fund (1984) *Quality Assessment in Health*. Maxwell, London.

3 An introduction to priority setting in the NHS

John Richards and Tony Lockett

This chapter provides a brief overview of the key issues involved in priority setting in the 'new NHS'. As priority setting has become increasingly topical at all levels of debate, political, professional and popular, it has spawned a huge body of literature and a proliferation of 'experts'. The subject is heavily laden with political and philosophical overtones and is thus both complex and emotive.

Priority setting, in its widest sense, is the process and rationale by which decisions are made on how to allocate resources in the face of many competing demands. The need to make these choices requires that there is a mechanism for determining which options have the greatest priority. This definition of priority setting rests on the assumption, familiar to economists, that demand is infinite and must be matched in some way to resources that are finite. The importance of this phenomenon to the NHS, and the widening gap between demand and the ability of resources to keep pace, was clearly expressed by Sir Brian Thwaites in 1987.[1]

Background

Recent interest in priority setting is set against a background of rising health care expenditure, both in the UK and world wide. Indeed the origins of the NHS reforms, embodied in the 1990 NHS and Community Care Act, may be traced to the financial crisis in the NHS that came to a head during 1988. Newspaper reports, such as one about a 'hole in the heart' baby who had died whilst waiting for an urgent operation in Birmingham, added fuel to the fire. Commentators put such problems down to a chronic shortage of resources, which had given rise to lengthy waiting lists and cancellations of theatre sessions due to a lack of skilled nursing staff. These events, amongst others, gave rise to the unprecedented step of a prime ministerial review in 1988 and culminated in the publication of the White Paper, *Working for Patients* in early 1989.[2] Rather than concluding that the solution was increased funding, as many had hoped, the review team opted for fundamental change in the management of the health service and sought to introduce an internal market to stimulate greater efficiency through the mechanism of competition. These market style reforms were inspired to a large degree by the work of an American academic, Alain Enthoven[3] (who had visited the UK in 1985) and by similar reforms in the education sector.

Critics of the government reforms suggested that the introduction of an internal market represented privatization of the NHS 'by the back door'. Nevertheless the White Paper and subsequent ministerial pronouncements expressed a clear commitment to the founding principles of the NHS: a system of health care funded mainly from general taxation and free at the point of delivery, and a comprehensive service providing equal access according to equal need. Whilst this appears clear, much of the subsequent complex debate ultimately comes down to these three key issues.

- What is the real meaning of a comprehensive service; does it mean everything that could be provided?

- What is meant by equal access according to equal need, and who defines what constitutes need as opposed to want?

- Can greater efficiency reconcile demand with available resources without compromising the fundamental principles of the NHS?

The international context

There is a truly international context to priority setting, which helps to put the UK experience in perspective. All health care systems, whether state funded or not, have been experiencing increasing pressure on resources, and many different approaches have been tried.[4] One of the most well known, but misquoted, examples is the Oregon Health Plan. The plan started by trying to rank over 700 categories of treatment according to cost utility criteria. This proved to be unworkable, and a second ranking method was devised based on 17 broad groupings of care from life-saving to cosmetic, but the approach was finally only approved when the problematical 'quality of life' criteria were ruled out. The plan has been through many changes and has been subject to considerable criticism, especially in the UK, where it has been seen by some as a bureaucratic and inequitable attempt to ration health care. However, the Oregon experiment[5] must be seen in the context of a health care system in which some 15% of the population had been excluded from the state welfare (Medicaid) system and could not afford private health care. The Oregon Health Plan's objective was to move from a situation of 'all health care for some' to 'some health care for all'. This is clearly different from the situation in the UK, where, since the creation of the NHS, we have had (at least) the illusion of a system providing all health care for all.

Despite these differences elements of the Oregon approach have been picked up in other countries, most notably Sweden and the UK. At the other end of the spectrum, countries such as New Zealand and the Netherlands have attempted to define a 'core' range of health services that should be state funded and to define criteria to limit access to care. Both have moved away from excluding specific procedures in favour of defining appropriate access to treatment through guidelines. The UK differs markedly from these other countries by not having any nationally determined approach to priority setting. Left largely to their own devices, health authorities in the UK have developed a variety of different approaches of widely varying style and sophistication. This variation itself has given rise, in the view of some, to inequitable variation in access to health care around the country, and this has attracted the interest of the House of Commons Health Select Committee.[6]

Looking below the surface

Public interest has continued as examples of rationing have attracted the attention of the media; from smokers being denied heart bypass surgery to infertile couples being denied access to *in vitro* fertilization. The case of 'child B', a leukaemia patient denied access to a second bone marrow transplant as a result of a clinical decision supported by Cambridge Health Authority, added a new twist to the debate as the health authority's decision was upheld in 1995 by the High Court[7]. In reality, however, cases such as this are but the tip of the iceberg as they represent only decisions not to provide specific treatments. In its widest sense, priority setting is part of every decision about how to spend money. This chapter will examine NHS priority setting as it occurs in three ways:

- market decisions: 'priority setting for purchasers'
- technocratic decisions: 'priority setting by clinicians'
- democratic decisions: 'the politics of priority setting'.

These distinctions are, of course, not pure and there is considerable overlap between them in practice.

Priority setting for purchasers

The NHS reforms place the responsibility upon district health authorities to assess health needs and purchase services accordingly. The separation of the purchasing and provision of health care introduced by the reforms has given rise to a greater awareness of decisions about how to spend resources by purchasers. Some say that this has meant that priority setting, or rationing as some prefer to describe it, has come out in the open.[8] They argue that rationing has always existed but is now more open to public scrutiny. In the past, they argue, rationing was conducted by clinicians at the bedside, i.e. implicitly. The creation of an internal market placed a greater responsibility for decisions about resource allocation on managers and others in purchasing authorities, provoking much debate about its appropriateness. The public, at least, seems to feel that doctors should decide. Doctors, on the other hand, feel that politicians should decide.[9] There seems to be little support for bureaucrats making the decisions, especially if they operate in 'quangos' that have no elected membership. This means that serious questions are posed about the accountability of decision making by health authorities, as it is indeed they who have, at district level, been making the decisions about resource allocation. In practice, however, historical patterns of investment have tended to dominate, and those changes that have occurred have been confined to the margin.

Faced with their new responsibilities, many health authorities turned naturally to economics in the search for a rational basis for making these choices. The techniques of cost benefit analysis, in varying degrees of sophistication, seemed to offer a basis for measuring the relative 'value for money' offered by different treatments. Thus some have suggested the use of league tables ranking the 'cost per QALY' of different interventions.[10] QALY stands for quality adjusted life years, a relatively crude measure that corrects post-treatment survival for the quality of that survival. In practice, quite apart from any philosophical or methodological difficulties in applying such devices to decision making, the proportion of health interventions for which such information is available makes these approaches of limited use. Thus, Klein and Redmayne[11] found that health authorities were making little use of such studies, and Robinson[12] called for a more pragmatic approach.

A further concern is that much economic analysis tends to assume that the aim is to deliver the optimal outcome for the population at large, the so-called utilitarian approach, which may mean that equity is compromised. In any case, there has been far from universal acceptance that such utilitarian approaches are necessary or appropriate. Some have argued that it is a mistake for health authorities to attempt to ration at a level of detail more appropriate to clinical decision making.[13] Others, most notably Hunter, have scorned attempts at explicit or rational decision making as unworkable and unethical. They have advocated, instead, the time-honoured process of 'muddling through elegantly'.[14]

Priority setting by clinicians

Quite a different approach to priority setting is represented by the development of management guidelines and protocols for 'appropriate' care, which is the preferred approach in New Zealand and the Netherlands. Guidelines generally involve attempts to define the criteria for access to specific types of treatment. The need for ownership by the clinicians who will use them (both hospital specialists and GPs) means that these must be developed locally and collaboratively. This can be a time-consuming and expensive process, and it will clearly be some time before protocols exist to cover the majority of health care, if this is indeed necessary.

It is not known how effective such protocols will be in reconciling demand with resources, as these protocols tend by their very nature to operate at the 'micro' and marginal level. Such protocols also carry with them the risk that they become merely a recipe for the status quo, as the participative approach tends to discourage the adoption of radical criteria.

A further problem with protocols is that, by defining who should have access to particular treatments, they may risk being discriminatory. Although generally defined in terms of 'ability to benefit', they may result in access being denied *de facto* on the grounds of age, life-style or other factors.

Moreover, all clinicians are familiar with priority setting on a daily basis with individual patients. They know well that the more articulate and informed patients are more demanding and that, as society changes, so too do people's expectations of the care that is appropriate to their needs.

Thus the apparently positive, scientific approach represented by clinical priorities cannot be divorced from the societal/cultural values on which such ideas of 'appropriateness' must be based.

The politics of priority setting

In response to these concerns, another school of thought has openly recognized priority setting as a political process and one which is inherently complex, with no right answers.[15] They advocate that health authorities should ensure that decisions are made as openly as possible and that they are based on values that either reflect public opinion or can be explained or justified when held to account. This approach has from time to time been supported in ministerial statements.[16,17] However, it is not without problems, perhaps the most significant being concerns about how properly to engage in an informed debate with the public and, linked to this, the difficulty in actually linking values to the decisions that are made.[18] In practice, it seems, it is probably only possible to take rational decision making so far before informed judgement, or 'gut feel', comes into play. This fact makes it difficult to avoid the criticism that explicitness and rationality are a sham, covering up vested interests and prejudice in the final analysis. However, the importance of these political factors in influencing decisions cannot be underestimated. Even the strongest advocates of rational decision making, the health economists, emphasize that their methods cannot by themselves produce decisions; they require a framework of values in order to determine the relative weight of different benefits.[19]

Practical, workable methods for priority setting by health authorities are very hard to find. One approach that has attracted interest in recent times, probably because it is a mechanism designed to balance priorities and to reconcile competing objectives, is that of programme budgeting (PB) or programme planning and budgeting systems (PPBS). This was a system developed for the US military, which rose to prominence in the late 1960s and early 1970s.[20] In simple terms, it involves the following steps.

1 Identify objectives.

2 Agree a programme format.

3 Identify timescales and indicators of programme efficiency.

4 Undertake a programme analysis of resource use.

5 Develop and compare options for achieving the objectives.

6 Collate information and report the findings to aid decision making.

In recent years, Mooney et al.[21] have advocated a modified form of PPBS, known as programme budgeting and marginal analysis (PBMA), as an aid to priority setting for health authorities. In essence, this involves building up 'wish lists' and ranking them in terms of their marginal cost benefit. Some health authorities, notably in mid-Glamorgan,[22] have tried this approach. However, given the current state of information about health services on which to base decisions, it remains problematical. An exercise using a modified form of PBMA was held in Southampton in 1994[18] and found that, of 49 options being examined, reliable cost utility data existed for only ten of them.

However, programme budgeting in some form may well have a future as it provides a framework for bringing together the three domains of market, technocratic and democratic decision making.

The future

Priority setting remains, therefore, fraught with problems and unresolved issues. The subject may have moved a step closer to respectability as a result of the detailed, thorough and well-balanced appraisal by the Health Select Committee in 1995.[6] The more emotive issues associated with priority setting, especially when expressed as rationing, have tended to be associated with concerns about the Conservative government's alleged 'hidden agenda' for privatization. This has tended to muddy the water. If there were to be a change of government, the fundamental challenges of priority setting would remain. In the long term a healthy public debate may indeed transpire, as it seems to have done in Oregon (Castanares, personal communication), where it is seen as inevitable and legitimate.

However, the view that priority setting is inevitable continues to be challenged by those who emphasize that the practice of health care remains, in many respects, quite inefficient and that rationing is therefore premature until these inefficiencies have been addressed.[23] Whilst true in many respects, this analysis tends to oversimplify the practicalities of improving efficiency and fundamentally misses the point that all decisions about how to spend money in a cash-limited system require choices to be made about which comes first.

A further challenge to the need for priority setting comes from the view that demand may not, in fact, be infinite. It is argued by some that, with overall NHS waiting times having been drastically reduced in recent years, we may be reaching a point where they become practically non-existent.[24]

However this argument misses the point that waiting lists are only one measure of demand for a relatively narrow spectrum of health care and ignores the possibility that some people in society who are in need may not get on to these waiting lists in the first place.

These considerations return the debate to the fundamental issues of equity in access to health services. Some moral philosophers have attacked the headlong rush towards utilitarian decision making by health authorities, claiming that this tends to mask health inequalities or even to discriminate against minorities.[25] At its simplest, to seek the greatest good for the greatest number may result in decisions whereby small numbers of individuals who are in great need may lose out whilst the majority have their relatively trivial needs met. Linked to these concerns is the increasing proportion of health care in the UK being funded privately. Yates' recent analysis of private work done by NHS consultants[26] challenges the notion that private health care relieves some of the burden on the NHS and further produces the worrying statistic that, whilst only one in ten people is privately insured, as many as one in four elective operations is being carried out privately.

A final twist in the tale of priority setting arises from the increasingly rapid development of GP fundholding as an alternative model of purchasing to health authorities. Government guidance[27] makes it clear that GP fundholding is expected to become the dominant form of purchasing in the future. As purchasing power shifts towards GPs as budget holders, this raises considerable doubt about health authorities' future role in priority setting. As GPs play an increasingly powerful role in setting priorities (ie. in making purchasing decisions), what values will they bring to bear? How will they be held to account for their decisions, and what mechanisms can they employ to give others a say? All of those problems that have beset health authorities remain just as relevant as the power shifts towards GPs. In an increasingly uncertain future, there remains little doubt that the dilemmas of priority setting will continue to vex the minds of policy makers, commentators, practitioners and the public.

References

1 Thwaites B (1987) *The NHS: The End of the Rainbow?* Foundation Lecture for University of Southampton Institute of Health Policy Studies. Wessex Regional Health Authority, Winchester.
2 Department of Health (1989) *Working for Patients* (Cmnd 555). HMSO, London.
3 Enthoven A C (1985) *Reflections on the Management of the National Health Service.* Occasional Paper No. 5. Nuffield Provincial Hospitals Trust, London.

4 Honigsbaum F, Calltorp J, Ham C et al. (1995) *Priority Setting Processes for Healthcare*. Radcliffe Medical Press, Oxford.

5 Honigsbaum F (1991) *Who Shall Live? Who Shall Die? Oregon's Health Financing Proposals*. King's Fund Institute, London.

6 House of Commons Health Select Committee (1995) *Priority Setting in the NHS: purchasing*. First report, Sessions 1994–95 (Cmnd 2826). HMSO, London.

7 *Health Service Journal*. News section. 16 March 1995.

8 Heginbotham C (1992) Rationing – Responses to Leading For Health. *BMJ*. 304:496–9.

9 BMJ (eds) (1993) *Rationing in Action*. BMJ, London.

10 Maynard A (1991) Developing the Health Care Market. *Economic Journal*. 101:1277–86.

11 Klein R and Redmayne S (1992) *Patterns of Priorities: A Study of the Purchasing and Rationing Policies of Health Authorities*. NAHAT Research Paper no. 7. NAHAT, Birmingham.

12 Robinson R (1994) The Policy Context. *BMJ*. 307:994–6.

13 Howell J B L (1992) Re-examining the Fundamental Principles of the NHS. *BMJ*. 304:297–9.

14 Hunter D J (1993) *Rationing Dilemmas in Healthcare*. NAHAT Research Paper no. 8. NAHAT, Birmingham.

15 Heginbotham C, Ham C, Cochrane M et al. (1992) *Purchasing Dilemmas*. King's Fund College Special Report. King's Fund Institute, London.

16 Bottomley V (1993) Priority Setting in the NHS. In *Rationing in Action* (eds BMJ), BMJ, London.

17 Department of Health (1995) *Government Response to the First Report from the Health Committee Session 1994–95* (Cmnd 2826). HMSO, London.

18 Honigsbaum F, Richards J and Lockett A (1995) *Priority Setting in Action: purchasing dilemmas*. Radcliffe Medical Press, Oxford.

19 Drummond M F (1993) The Contribution of Health Economics to Cost Effective Health Care Delivery. In *Purchasing and Providing Cost Effective Health Care* (eds M F Drummond and A Maynard), Churchill Livingstone, Edinburgh.

20 Carlson J (1970) The Status and Next Steps for Planning Programming and Budgeting. In *Policy Experience and Analysis* (ed. J Wildavsky), Markham Publishers, New York.

21 Mooney G H, Gerrard K, Donaldson C et al. (1992) Priority Setting in Purchasing: Some Practical Guidelines. NAHAT Research Paper no. 6. NAHAT, Birmingham.

22 Cohen D (1994) Marginal Analysis in Practice: An Alternative to Needs Assessment for Contracting Health Care. *BMJ*. 309:781–5.

23 Roberts C, Crosby D, Dunn R et al. (1995) Rationing is a Desperate Measure. Open Space. *Health Service Journal*. 12 January 1995.

24 Weiner D and Ferris J (1993) *GP Fundholding: Lessons from America*. Report no. 7. King's Fund Institute, London.

25 Doyal L (1995) How not to ration health care: the moral perils of utilitarian decision making. In *Priority Setting in Action: purchasing dilemmas* (eds F Honigsbaum, J Richards and A Lockett), Radcliffe Medical Press, Oxford.

26 Yates J (1995) *Dispatches: Serving Two Masters*. Channel Four Television, London.

27 NHS Executive (1994) *Developing NHS Purchasing and GP Fundholding*. Executive Letter (94)79. DoH, Leeds.

4 What is NHS purchasing, and where is it going?

Tony Shaw and Murray Cochrane

The purchasing of health care in the NHS is still relatively new. The NHS reforms officially brought the process into being in April 1991. From that date money was allocated to NHS purchasers, typically DHAs, according to the size and health indicators of the resident population, so that care could be bought to meet the health needs of local people.

Nationally less attention was given to purchasing in its early days than to provider units, which were undergoing dramatic changes. NHS Trusts were being set up as the new provider organizations. However, as they became accepted, the spotlight turned towards purchasing. The challenge was whether purchasing could enhance health improvement.

Purchasing developments have taken place at breakneck speed. Experiments and innovation one year have become established practice the next. For example, early contracts for health care necessarily reflected a 'steady state', but these were soon replaced by bolder market testing and limited use of the private sector. GP fundholders flexed their purchasing muscle and secured improvements in the quality of services, in some cases using their funds to provide more care in their own practices. At each stage managers in the NHS have been able to innovate and compare their advances with colleagues elsewhere in the country.

Purchasing successes

The achievements that have been associated with the development of purchasing, but are not necessarily all a direct result of it, illustrate the impact it can have in improving health services.

- Waiting times have been driven down to all-time lows, maximum waits being under 12 months in many parts of the country.

- Many new Patient's Charter standards have been met by using a combination of investment and influence (Box 4.1).

Box 4.1: The Patient's Charter

Key priorities

- Waiting times, inpatients and outpatients
- Accident and emergency: immediate assessment
- Outpatients: seen within 30 minutes
- Cancelled operations: readmitted within one month
- GP practice charters

Rights and standards: examples

- Complaints: prompt responses
- Privacy, dignity and respect

Recent developments

- Catering
- Mixed sex wards
- Maternity charter
- Charter for children and young people

- The replacement of Victorian institutions for mental health and learning disability clients is taking place faster than in the past, with the rapid growth of community-based care, often with considerable social services collaboration.

- Primary care services have been boosted by making more care, for example physiotherapy, more complex diagnostic procedures, outpatient clinics and chiropody, available in GP surgeries.

- Contracts are being switched between facilities to achieve higher quality services at a lower price, and are often moved to locations closer to the people served.

- Health gain is no longer just a theoretical notion: local health strategies and *The Health of the Nation*[1] targets are directing efforts towards measurable improvements in accident services and the prevention of coronary heart disease and cancer.

● The effectiveness and outcomes of treatment are being much more rigorously evaluated to convince purchasers of their worth. Patterns of care are consequently changing, as seen in, for example, the shift from hospital to community-based maternity care.

None of these changes would have been implemented as rapidly without the introduction of health care purchasing. Even more dramatic has been the associated culture changes; the professionally-led pressure group culture is increasingly balanced with the wider recognition of the need for improvements to be based on good quality evidence.

How purchasing works

Knowing what to buy: strategy development

Figure 4.1 summarizes the key steps in the purchasing process. The health status of the population is the start and endpoint. The indicators of health, whether in terms of mortality, years of life lost before the age of 75 or loss of social functioning, define both the challenge for purchasers and how successful they have been. For all DHAs the Director of Public Health's annual report is the key reference point for the health status of the local people.

Purchasers have specific targets to aim for in the high profile areas set out in *The Health of the Nation* (Box 4.2).[1] In addition, most purchasers have identified their own local set of health targets against which to measure progress.

Box 4.2: *Health of the Nation* priority areas

● Coronary heart disease and stroke

● Cancer

● Mental health

● HIV/AIDS and sexual health

● Accidents

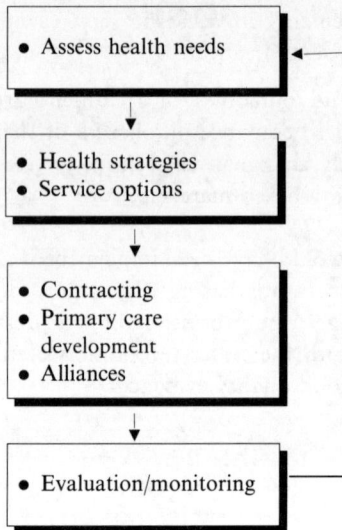

Figure 4.1: Health care commissioning.

Having assessed health needs, the next step is to prepare strategies for meeting them. This involves designing a service profile that reflects good practice and is based on best evidence.

The views of users and carers become particularly important at this stage of drawing up purchasing plans. Collaboration with a wide range of 'stakeholders' is essential. Purchasers cannot work in isolation. They must have long term partnerships with providers, fundholding and non-fundholding GPs, social services, other agencies and the private and voluntary sectors.

Figure 4.2 illustrates the key influences on purchasing and the balance that must be struck between competing priorities. National policies and targets from above have to be balanced with pressures from local providers and health care professionals. The potential for collaboration with co-purchasers such as GP fundholders and local authorities has to be taken into account, as must consumer influences from the local community. Ultimately, however, it is the purchaser who must decide priorities on behalf of all the local stakeholders.

Strategies do not stand still. As the capacity of primary and community care grows and as new technologies are developed, so the strategies, and the patterns of care that they promote, will change. The full potential of looking across the whole spectrum of primary, secondary and tertiary care has yet to be tapped, as have the possibilities, and the potential pitfalls, of pooling health and social care resources.

National and regional:
Policies and targets

Collaboration:

DHA
FHSA/GPs
Social services
Local authorities
Voluntary/private sector

Purchasing decisions

Consumer influences:

Individuals
Community Health Councils
Carers
Relatives
Interest groups

Service
contracts

Providers and health professionals:

Hospital
Community services
GPs
Voluntary/private sector

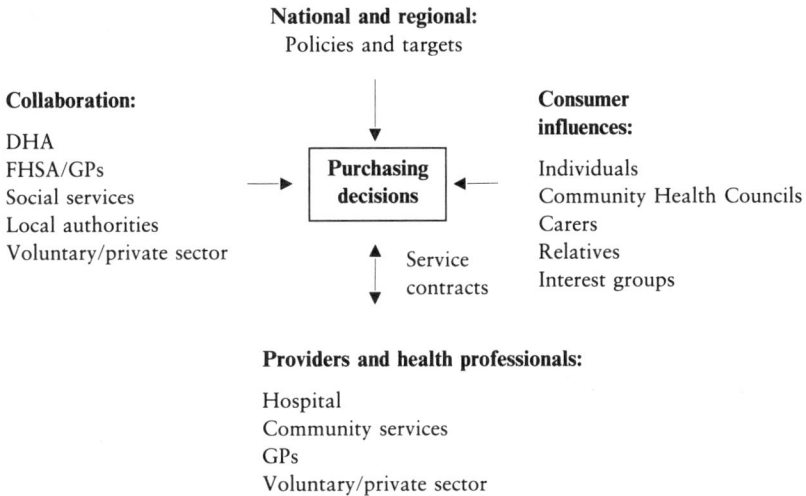

Figure 4.2: Influences on purchasing.

The financial plan determines whether a strategy is realistic or a 'wish list'. It demonstrates that strategies can be achieved and provides a clear signal of the priorities attached to particular health programmes.

Health economics has become increasingly relevant for purchasers. Skills in evaluating cost-effectiveness are being used to help set priorities for future services. Financial planning is being employed to identify how efficiency savings can be found and to ensure that resources from different agencies are applied appropriately.

Turning strategy into action: the contracting process

Contracting has been variously described as the 'engine room' of purchasing and the 'means not the end'. Initially, it was thought that everything achieved by a purchaser would be defined, at some stage, in a contract. However, the breadth of opportunities open to purchasers has widened and with it the definition of purchasing from simply 'buying' to cover all aspects of 'commissioning'. Commissioning encompasses positive alliances with other agencies and the wider community, and activities such as influencing research and development and encouraging audit programmes. It also includes facilitating developments in primary care, in voluntary action and community care. Often such facilitating is also accompanied by an investment to the provider organizations concerned, however small.

Contracts specify the service required, including the key elements of quality, cost and volume of service. Quality can be defined in terms of Patient's Charter[2] standards, such as waiting times, or ensure that processes, such as audit or complaints procedures, are in place. As contracts become more sophisticated, the possibility of using outcomes of treatment as criteria are being explored.

Outcome measures may be expressed in terms of, for example, death rates from appendicitis and peptic ulcers. Alternatively a process can be used as a 'proxy' for an outcome. For example a target for childhood immunization rates could be used in place of other measures of child health. The extent to which outcome measures come into use will depend on purchasers and providers gaining confidence in the measures being devised.

Contracts are costed through a process of negotiation that hinges on the relative importance of factors such as quality and volume of service. Extensive efforts have been made to refine the approach to the costing of contracts. The maxims have to be applied of 'price must equal cost' and 'no cross-subsidization between contracts'. Capital charges made against providers' physical assets have become an integral element in contract prices to ensure that purchasing decisions are made with an understanding of the full cost of a service.

Volume of service is often defined in terms of the level of activity required, such as the expected number of finished consultant episodes, outpatient attendances or community nurse contacts. Activity levels and quality are of critical interest to purchasers in ensuring that value for money is achieved.

'Extracontractual referrals' are those made by GPs for treatments not covered by a contract. For example, patients may be referred for bone marrow transplants to distant specialist providers or there may be referrals for courses of residential psychotherapy. Extracontractual referrals have proved to be the most difficult part of a purchasing budget to control. Many purchasers have had to limit approvals for referrals outside contracts, and this has tested relationships with referring GPs.

After much controversy the right of hospital specialists to make tertiary referrals to another specialty or to a more specialized centre without seeking the prior approval of the relevant purchaser has been granted as part of national contracting guidance.

Three major types of contract were set out initially for the NHS: block contracts, which give access to a defined range of services for a fixed price; cost and volume contracts, in which part of the contract sum is dependent on the level of activity achieved; and cost per case contracts, where an agreed price is paid for each procedure, and the number of procedures carried out determines the amount of money paid.

As contracting has developed, so the 'currency' of contracts has changed. 'Health care resource groups', or groups of procedures, are being considered for use as a standard tool for defining the content of a contract. In addition, more sophisticated block contracts have been developed to include 'triggers' (more money is paid if activity exceeds a certain level) and 'incentive payments' (more money is paid if certain standards are achieved, such as a maximum waiting time of nine months for surgery).

Measuring performance: evaluation and monitoring

The evaluation and monitoring stage of the commissioning process can include a review of a wide range of factors, including:

- the achievement of health targets (such as reductions in mortality) or intermediate goals, such as screening targets
- the effectiveness of treatment in improving the health status of the population
- waiting times against national and local targets
- improvements in the quality of clinical care demonstrated through the audit process or Patient's Charter[2] reports
- financial control, such as monitoring the expenditure on extracontractual referrals
- the performance of 'care in the community', such as the number of patients awaiting discharge from hospital or the completion of transfers to community-based care from long-stay institutions
- comparisons with best practice and audit reports, for example the level of day surgery carried out.

Commissioning across primary and secondary care

One of the first challenges for NHS purchasing was how the services of GPs, dentists, opticians and pharmacists within primary care should be brought into the purchaser–provider system. FHSAs were seen as both purchasers and providers of services. Despite this informal health commissions began to be formed, which brought together FHSAs and DHAs. The move was sanctioned formally in legislation in 1995, which enabled the creation of new combined health authorities from April 1996.

Commissioning across primary and secondary care opens up the exciting opportunity of being able to look at health care provision as a whole, wherever it takes place, be it in the GP's surgery or the specialist hospital. The traditional divide between the management of hospital and family health services will therefore be reduced.

In practice what does it mean?

Perhaps the most significant advantage of commissioning across primary and secondary care is that resources can be placed where the greatest benefit can be achieved. If the money available to FHSAs and DHAs is pooled, resources can support beneficial strategic shifts of care away from secondary (or hospital care) to primary care. Services such as physiotherapy, occupational therapy, dietetics and midwifery may, as a consequence, be more likely to be provided in GP practices, other community facilities and the patient's own home, rather than in the traditional hospital or institutional setting.

In specialties such as dermatology and urology, consultants are holding outpatient clinics in GP surgeries, and a greater number of similar services may be provided in this setting. Diagnostic specialties, such as radiology and pathology, are becoming more accessible to GPs, either because a facility has been provided near the surgery or because of direct access to hospital facilities. Many of the innovations in primary care are being led by GP fundholders who have been able to invest their funds in services within their practices, rather than referring patients to hospital.

FHSAs fund a proportion of the cost of practice nurses employed by non-fundholding GPs. DHAs purchase community nursing from community NHS trusts, which then employ health visitors and district nurses to work alongside GP practices. Being able to look at the total investment in community nursing, wherever it has traditionally been funded from, should ensure a better distribution of nursing resources to meet the needs in each area.

A further example of the benefits of joint purchasing can be seen in prescribing, one of the largest variable cost elements of the NHS. Instead of cost-shifting occurring for medicines from cash-limited hospitals to non-cash-limited GPs, health commissions can encourage more cost-effective prescribing by GPs at the same time as promoting policies in hospital prescribing that are consistent with this. The current tendency to shift costs is not always in the best interests of patients and can lead to difficulties over which doctor supervises their clinical management.

The plans published by NHS purchasers each year are increasingly showing how investment is being applied across primary and secondary care. At the same time it has been recognized that there is a need for research evidence to back up the emphasis on primary care. Purchasers are influencing research and development programmes to fill this gap.

Moves towards a 'primary care-led NHS' are underway. The expansion of GP fundholding is being coupled with a redefined role for the new health authorities. Nationally GP fundholding is expected to cover 50% of the population by 1996 through one of the three options available:

- community fundholding, covering a limited range of community health services

- standard fundholding, which covers a range of inpatient and outpatient procedures across hospital and community health services; this excludes, for example, complex treatments, inpatient mental health and maternity care

- total purchasing, which enables groups of GP practices to purchase the full range of health care for their population, including, for example complex treatments, mental health and maternity care.

The 50% coverage of GP fundholding will result in approximately 20% of NHS resources being allocated to GP fundholders. A significant role remains for the new health authorities to purchase directly the remaining 80% of health care and to carry out their role of:

- strategy development

- monitoring of performance

- support for GP fundholders.

An accountability framework has been published by the NHSE which aims to define the relationship between GP fundholders and health authorities and places requirements on GP fundholders, such as the preparation of health plans and annual reports on performance.

Measuring purchasing performance

How is the success of purchasing judged? In a series of speeches former Health Minister Brian Mawhinney[3] set out seven 'hallmarks' of good purchasing:

1   a strategic view

2   robust contracts

3   knowledge-based decisions

4   responsiveness to local people

5   mature relations with providers

6   local alliances

7   organizational fitness.

The short-term performance of purchasers is often assessed against immediate priorities such as efficiency gains, reduced waiting times, control of prescribing costs and achievement of Patient's Charter standards, including, for
example, the number of individual charters developed within general practice.

Targets for efficiency gains (using an efficiency index) have been adopted
by the Treasury as a favoured tool for negotiating the NHS annual financial
settlement. The 'efficiency index' is used each year to measure the increase in
clinical activity secured for a certain level of financial resources. It is widely
regarded in the NHS as a blunt tool. For example it is not consistent with the
drive to promote primary and community care, which feature in the index
only to a limited extent.

In the widest sense the success of NHS purchasers should be judged
against their progress towards health improvement. However, the health
measures available, such as the reductions in death rates set out in *The
Health of the Nation*,[1] take a long time to achieve, and many of the current
health outcome indicators are dependent on the actions of individuals and
agencies outside the NHS. Health status is a complex topic and related to
non-NHS factors such as social status, housing, the environment and
individual risk factors, for example smoking, alcohol consumption and diet.
Nonetheless the trend towards measuring health outcomes more precisely
and thus being able to quantify health improvement is gathering pace.

The future of NHS purchasing

Looking ahead some form of purchaser–provider system is likely to continue
in the NHS, whichever political party is in power. If there is political change,
the contrast may show in relation to such features as whether GP fund-

holding is expanded or abandoned, whether NHS trusts maintain their independence and whether local authority appointees have places on NHS boards.

Exciting opportunities lie ahead for NHS purchasing. New purchasing authorities to be formed from FHSAs and DHAs will strengthen commissioning. For the first time in the history of the NHS, purchasers will routinely be taking an overall view across the full spectrum of health care.

The pressure for changes to the GP contract may lead to more experimentation, with local contracts between GP practices and NHS purchasers for a range of services.

In community health services, primary care and social care, complex interrelationships will become an increasing challenge for purchasers.

In acute care, purchasing will need to support the radical restructuring of hospital services in major cities and the trends towards more day surgery, new techniques, expanding demand from an ageing population and higher expectations from consumers.

In an environment of constant change, NHS purchasing can make a unique contribution to shaping the future direction of health and social care and improving the nation's health.

References

1 Secretary of State for Health (1991) *Health of the Nation*. HMSO, London.
2 Secretary of State for Health (1991) *The Patient's Charter* (part of The Citizen's Charter). HMSO, London.
3 NHS Management Executive (1993) *Purchasing for Health: A Framework for Action*. Speeches by Dr B Mawhinney and Sir Duncan Nichol. NHSME, London.

5   Marketing in the NHS

Andrew Boon

'Everyone lives by selling something'
Robert Louis Stevenson

Until very recently marketing was an alien concept in the NHS. The emphasis was on curtailing costs by constraining demand; rationing by queues and waiting lists. The analogies with old-style Soviet bloc economic practices are obvious. In theory, at least, we had a standard product and a uniform service, and if quality sometimes left a lot to be desired, we were expected to be grateful that we were getting it cheaply! Such systems are set up for the benefit of staff rather than customers. Marketing has little to offer in these circumstances.

The world has changed. The collectivist attitudes developed in the 1930s, strengthened by the demands of national organization for world war and incorporated into the NHS at its inception, have weakened. Meek acceptance of medical, or indeed institutional, authority is less common, and individualist consumerist attitudes prevail. People are increasingly demanding more and better and, if able to, are prepared to pay for high quality.

The introduction of internal NHS markets is one consequence of this 'paradigm shift' in society. It has provided NHS hospitals with strong incentives to develop marketing skills. It is becoming clear that purchaser decisions are favouring those who carry out the most effective marketing. No hospital can ignore marketing principles and expect to survive.

This chapter examines what marketing means, whether marketing principles are applicable to public sector bodies such as the NHS and how to go about developing a market-oriented organization.

Why have a market?

In common with the economics of the former Soviet bloc, the NHS was 'production-oriented'. Production orientation occurs where goods and services are planned and produced with greater regard for accumulated management experience, established production techniques and current

labour force skills than for the actual or potential preferences of users.[1] In
the context of the NHS, this has led to various professional groups, notably
doctors, pursuing their own individual concepts of patient need with scant
regard for the health demands of the community. Enthoven, amongst others,
has argued that the structure of the NHS lacks strong incentives for the
improvement of care and services, that existing incentives for improvement
operate in a perverse fashion and that the end result is lower quality and
inefficient use of resources.[2]

In order to address these concerns, and in keeping with its philosophy that
industry can provide effective models through which to improve the
management of public section organizations, government introduced the
concept of an internal NHS market.[3] DHAs and GP fundholders were to
become selective 'purchasers' of services from 'provider' units. Providers
would in turn need to be sensitive to the underlying reasons for any changes
in the market for their services and would plan accordingly. In other words
providers would become 'market-oriented'.[1]

Consequently marketing should be of fundamental concern to any service
'provider' operating within the NHS. This applies not only at the level of the
district general or teaching hospital but also to individual functional units
within acute hospitals. The introduction of clinical budgeting and internal
contracting for services will have particular implications for 'support'
specialties, notably anaesthetics, radiology and pathology.[4] Just as DHAs
are no longer under any obligation to 'purchase' only from themselves (or
their former directly-managed units), so support services cannot assume that
medical and surgical directorates will continue to place their contracts 'in
house'. Neighbouring units might offer facilities of higher quality at lower
cost. However the opportunities offered, and threats posed, by the operation
of the market apply to all clinical specialties. Effective marketing is the key to
success in this new environment.

What is marketing?

Marketing is not a euphemism for selling or advertising, although it may
incorporate these activities.[1] The word 'marketing' is used in three
interrelated but distinct contexts. First, it describes a business philosophy,
often termed the 'marketing concept'. Businesses that adopt a marketing
concept can be described as 'user-oriented', 'market-oriented' or 'customer
focused' and operate according to two fundamental principles.

1   In every phase of its operations, the organization must bring itself into mutually satisfactory relationships with the users of its products and services.

2   Based on this pattern of relationships, it must then strive for an adequate return on its own investment in providing these products or services.

This outward-facing philosophy, towards the wants and needs of users rather than inward, towards what an organization likes doing or is experienced in doing, characterizes the marketing concept. It has been constantly emphasized by Tom Peters[5] amongst others as the hallmark of successful companies, and a fundamental aspect of TQM.[6] It is essentially an attitude of mind, the opposite of saying, 'This is what we make, buy some'.

Marketing is also a management process. It anticipates customer requirements, identifying and satisfying their wants/needs by providing the right product or service at the right price, time and place.

Third, marketing is a collective term for a series of techniques used to carry out the process. These include research, product planning, pricing, distribution and promotion (which incorporates advertising and selling). Such considerations (often called the seven 'Ps' – product, price, place, promotion, people, processes and physical resources) constitute marketing tactics, which are employed in various combinations (the 'marketing mix') in a 'marketing strategy' to achieve 'marketing objectives'.

Although marketing may at first sight appear foreign to NHS employees, many of us carry out marketing without ever being aware of doing so. Most would agree that success in job interviews is entirely dependent on marketing oneself as a candidate. Those in the medical profession who protest most loudly and publicly against the market concept are often those who have been the most successful 'marketeers' in their own careers. Likewise, a teaching hospital unit with an international reputation may in reality offer no better a service to patients than does a neighbouring district general hospital (DGH) department. It might simply have carried out more effective marketing.

Who is the customer?

The customer is central to the marketing philosophy.[1] Markets may be composed of very large numbers of customers (a 'mass market') or relatively small groups with specific requirements (a 'market segment'). Whatever the market composition, it is crucial to identify the customer, defined as the person or organization buying the goods or services. In the context of the NHS, the DHA or GP fundholder is the customer of provider units (such as the hospital Trusts) who in turn may be customers when purchasing specialist or support services. Most importantly, the customer is not the patient. Health care is purchased on behalf of the patient (often termed the 'user'). Possibly for political reasons, this fundamental distinction is fudged in many official communications.[7,8]

Purchasing decisions are susceptible to user pressures. Patients may be able to affect purchasing decisions by complaining about the perceived quality of their care by provider units to the purchaser. Clearly this will have a greater impact if the purchaser is a GP fundholder rather than a remote DHA. The closer the purchaser–patient relationship, the more effectively the internal market will operate in the patient's interests. While marketing efforts must be directed primarily at purchasers, therefore, it should be noted that marketing a service to patients may indirectly influence certain purchasers.

Is there a marketing culture in the NHS?

Chaston has stated that the behaviour of an organization is guided and influenced by the values and attitudes of the employees, called the organizational culture.[9] The first and most crucial stage in market-oriented strategic planning is to ensure that an organization has a culture that is sympathetic to a customer-focused approach. If cultural change is necessary to become market-oriented, this must take place at all levels of the organization and cannot be achieved by managerial edict. However, many private sector companies have succeeded in creating a new market-oriented culture from unpromising beginnings. Public sector organizations, in contrast, have had comparatively limited success. There are a number of possible reasons, including:

- the gap between expectations and perception
- the dominance of professionals
- hierarchical bureaucratic management
- inadequate information and accounting systems.

The first problem encountered lies in matching service expectations against perceptions. To overpromise and underdeliver is a constant danger in cash-limited public sector organizations attempting to become customer-focused.

A further problem relates to the staffing of public sector organizations. Most include large numbers of professionals. Such groups tend to have had prolonged, specialized training, to value expertise and technical ability above organizational objectives, to identify most closely with other members of their profession and to have a generally low level of loyalty to any particular employer. They may frustrate market-oriented strategies through their reluctance to work in cross-functional teams. They need to be convinced of the benefits.

Professionals tend to react adversely to hierarchical management systems, which are perceived as demeaning to their professional status. Complaints that 'managerialism' is replacing 'professionalism' in the NHS may indicate that many NHS managers, in characteristic public sector fashion, are inappropriately attempting to install rigid bureaucratic structures.[10] Current situations demand the creation of flatter organizations, with delegation of decision making to the lowest possible level. The dominant professional ethos in the NHS provides ideal conditions for developing successful flat hierarchies. What is often lacking is trust.

Public sector accounting systems have been geared towards keeping expenditure within a specific allocated budget; it was seldom possible to identify accurate costs attributable to specific activities. Consequently the wider, more appropriate use of information technology has been identified as a priority. The provision of timely and accurate information is crucial to effective marketing.

What is marketing strategy?

Strategic planning lies at the heart of marketing (Figure 5.1). It has been defined as 'a process whereby organizations determine their current situation relative to market conditions and internal capabilities and use this inform-ation to develop specifications for their future direction'.[1] The process involves the assessment of strategic alternatives and should increase the like-lihood of achieving business objectives. It is most important that marketing planning takes account of the organization's fundamental purpose, its 'mission statement', otherwise, there is a risk of being sidetracked into peripheral issues. The results should be:

- greater staff commitment

- a broader perspective of the entire service
- integration of the work of different sections/departments
- a clear understanding of priorities
- increased responsiveness to customer needs.

Marketing planning is an imprecise exercise; there are no right or wrong answers. There is a false assumption that the most successful planning results from the availability of very extensive market information and the

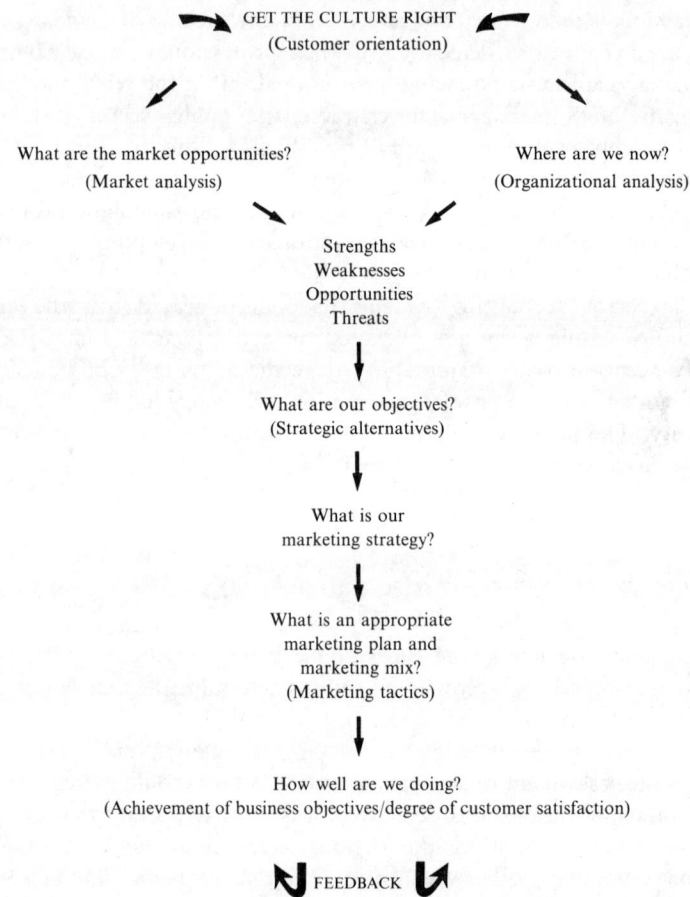

GET THE CULTURE RIGHT
(Customer orientation)

What are the market opportunities?   Where are we now?
(Market analysis)   (Organizational analysis)

Strengths
Weaknesses
Opportunities
Threats

What are our objectives?
(Strategic alternatives)

What is our
marketing strategy?

What is an appropriate
marketing plan and
marketing mix?
(Marketing tactics)

How well are we doing?
(Achievement of business objectives/degree of customer satisfaction)

FEEDBACK

Figure 5.1: Marketing planning and implementation.

application of extremely sophisticated analytic techniques. However this philosophy ignores the inherent unpredictability of markets that behave in non-linear or 'chaotic' ways.[11] It is probably a more effective use of resources to employ simple techniques, but constantly review strategy in the light of experience.

The first task is to analyse both the market opportunities and internal competence to satisfy market needs and ask the question, 'Where are we now?'

Audit of internal competence should focus on:

- communication with customers

- influence of customers

- appropriateness of management structures.

Marketing analysis examines services currently provided and attempts to predict future needs. It makes use of marketing research, defined as 'the systematic gathering, recording and analysing of data about problems relating to the marketing of goods and services'. It is important to identify:

- the services provided

- the purchase criteria

- the customers

- the competition

- relevant externalities.

The first and most important consideration is to be clear about what the hospital/directorate is in business to do. Each individual service must be studied and its distinctive characteristics noted (a 'service profile').[12] Their marketing requirements might be radically different. If possible a 'unique selling point' (USP) should be identified. This may often influence purchasing decisions when every competitor is uniformly offering a 'high-quality service'.

The reasons for purchasing decisions are often complex; decisions are not always made for reasons that purchasers are willing to state publicly or even admit to themselves. The price of the service is an important and obvious factor. In the long-term it is unlikely that purchasers will pay substantially higher prices for a similar service obtainable elsewhere for less. However, inertia is a common reason why this may occur in the short-term; historical patterns of purchase may be difficult to overcome. Loyalty to a particular service provider can also be due to personal or political ties. Cynics might argue that many surprising purchasing decisions can be traced back to the nineteenth hole of the local golf club!

'Quality' is frequently cited as the justification for purchasing decisions that appear to ignore price differentials. Quality is a subjective concept, largely related to customer satisfaction. Clearly when attempting to attract new business, existing customer satisfaction is less relevant; marketing must then rely on the creation and promotion of a 'quality image'.

It is most important to assess customer attitudes towards services currently provided, together with their preferences for future service development. This is classical market research, which can be carried out using a wide variety of techniques. These include personal interviewing, postal surveys, telephone enquiries, panel research and group interviews. Common to all is the need for careful planning to achieve maximum value from the activity.

Identification of current and potential competitors is another important aspect of market analysis. Their relative strengths and weaknesses should be scrutinized in order to identify areas of market opportunity. This is fundamental to 'SWOT' (strengths, weaknesses, opportunities and threats) analysis. Such competitors may be direct (e.g. other NHS providers) or indirect (e.g. new technology).

'Perfect' markets are not affected by externalities; all real markets are, and the health care market is probably affected more than any other. These externalities included political, environmental, sociological and technological factors. The study of their impact on marketing strategy is often termed 'PEST' analysis.

Apart from familiar techniques such as SWOT and PEST analysis, marketing theory makes extensive use of other tools.[9] For example whether to attempt to win a mass market or take a focused approach can be represented as a matrix against the alternatives of price competition or service differentiation (strategic positioning matrix (Table 5.1)). Similarly a directional policy matrix relates the ability to satisfy customers in a range of services to the degree of opportunity to deliver customer satisfaction (Table 5.2). Ultimately this analysis should enable an organization to generate appropriate strategic marketing objectives. These must, of course, be co-ordinated with the objectives of other departments, including finance and personnel. The next stage is implementation.

How are marketing objectives achieved?

Marketing objectives are achieved through the use of 'marketing tactics'. The 'mix' of tactics used constitutes the marketing strategy. Classically, the

Table 5.1: Strategic positioning matrix

Coverage	Competitive position	
	Cost leadership	Differentiation
Mass market	Cost-based market domination (usually lowest price)	Performance-based differentiation (perceived or real)
Focused	Focused cost leadership	Specialist position differentiation

Table 5.2: Directional policy matrix

Ability to satisfy customers		Opportunity to satisfy customers		
		Low 3	Average 7	High 10
	0			
Low	0	Immediate withdrawal	Phased withdrawal	Worth a try (but be ready to pull out!)
Average	3	Phased withdrawal	Maintain position	Invest to enhance ability
High	7	Reduce investment	Invest to diversify	Invest to retain lead
	10			

tactics employed are the seven 'Ps' of service marketing:

- product
- price
- promotion
- place
- people
- processes
- physical resources

The 'products' of health care organizations (defined by Theodore Levitt as a 'complex cluster of value satisfactions') are an enormously complex mixture of services. However, most competitors are able to provide an almost identical range of services. In such circumstances continuous innovation is necessary to gain a market lead, and USPs are useful. USPs may reflect real product differentiation, although this is not strictly necessary; the perception of the customer is the crucial thing.

Price is not the same as cost. Marketing research should have established the price that the market will pay for a given service (and whether price is an important factor in the purchase decision). The cost may be very different. However, in the current, fairly primitive and closely regulated NHS market, price and cost have to be closely linked. There are clear rules governing how prices are calculated and in what circumstances marginal costs can be used. 'Loss leaders' are strongly discouraged (although not unknown).

The primary purpose of promotion is to convey information. Promotion of a service or organization can encompass a wide range of activities. These include advertising, public relations, demonstrations and personal selling. Promotion can be an expensive and time-consuming exercise, which consequently needs to be targeted at specific customer groups. Promotion can be subtle or disguised, a fact not often acknowledged by those who refuse to admit to ever being influenced by 'advertising'.

Considerations of place, in a marketing sense, include service location and the logistics of service delivery. Obvious options for any hospital to explore are the possibility of providing services off-site, whether in GP practices or in the patient's home. In many specialties (e.g. care of the elderly) this has always formed a component of the workload. The trend can be expected to accelerate. When patients have to travel to hospitals, ease of access is important. We are moving from an era of large hospitals with small car parks to one of small hospitals with large car parks!

It is crucial for any organization wishing to become market-oriented to involve all grades of staff in the strategy. A marketing philosophy cannot be successfully imposed from the top. Tactics must include the establishment of effective two-way communication channels. Important decisions should not automatically be made in camera; freedom of information must be the guiding principle. Staff may also need retraining in practical skills more relevant to the market (e.g. in computers or customer relations). A particularly important role is that of marketing manager.

'Processes' refers to the activities and procedures associated with adding value to the various provision tasks. This includes devising efficient, responsive work patterns; establishing appropriate management structures with clear lines of responsibility and accountability; ensuring effective communications within the hospital and with external customers; and closely integrating support services with the technical and professional work of each department.

Finally, marketing tactics include consideration of the actual physical resources required to undertake the various services. A constant theme must be to relate each acquisition to the needs of the market. If capital resources are insufficient for large purchases, leasing arrangements are an obvious solution. This approach, common in the private sector, is often overlooked in the NHS.

Monitoring and review

Marketing is not a 'one-off' process. Progress towards objectives needs to be monitored, and changes in tactics made when necessary. The entire strategy must continually adapt to changing market circumstances. The views of customers should be regularly sought, and the results fed back into the planning process. By establishing a dialogue with customers, services should become precisely matched to purchaser requirements, ensuring the efficient use of resources for mutual benefit.

Conclusions

Most NHS employees react negatively to 'marketing'. They should not. Marketing is about strengthening purchaser–provider relationships, making the best use of resources and benefiting patients. Adoption of marketing principles and practice will raise quality, ensure cost-effectiveness and accelerate the introduction of new developments. Conversely services that do not meet customer requirements can be quickly run down. Overall services should develop in line with customer priorities and truly reflect the health needs of the community.

References

1 Frain J (1981) *Introduction to Marketing*. MacDonald and Evans, Plymouth.
2 Berwick D M, Enthoven A and Bunker J P (1992) Quality Management in the NHS: The Doctor's Role – I. *BMJ*. 304: 235–9.

3 Department of Health (1989) *Working for Patients* (Cmnd 555). HMSO, London.
4 Christie J L (1992) Lessons for the NHS. II: Confusion in the Market Place. *ACP News* (Autumn): 5–8.
5 Peters T (1989) *Thriving on Chaos: Handbook for a Management Revolution*. Pan, London.
6 Berwick D M, Enthoven A and Bunker J P (1992) Quality Management in the NHS: The Doctor's Role – II. *BMJ*. 304: 304–8.
7 Owens J and McGill J (1993) *Marketing in the NHS: Putting Patients First*. NAHAT, Birmingham.
8 Hawley A and Ferguson A (1992) *Marketing in the National Health Service*. NHS Wales, Cardiff.
9 Chaston I (1993) *Customer-focused Marketing*. McGraw-Hill, Maidenhead.
10 Charlton B (1992) Underlying Trends in the Health Service: A Master Theory. *BMJ*. 306: 562.
11 Gleick J (1988) *Chaos: Making a New Science*. Penguin Books, Middlesex.
12 Webster D (1991) Produce a Service Specification. *BMJ*. 302: 1450–1.

6 Casemix, coding and contracting: a beginner's guide

Peter Lees and Paul Stafford

The 1990s have seen major changes in the management of the NHS, with the advent of a number of new processes for the 'commissioning' of health care. Priority setting has been introduced to reconcile the competing demands for health care within a population and to rationalize the allocation of resources. Purchasing and the internal market are providing the framework to procure health care through the contracting process and to obtain the best value for money. The contracting process is the mechanism for purchasers to negotiate who provides what health care, how much of it and at what cost. To enable 'purchasers' and 'providers' to engage in this process, and to ensure that the 'money follows the patient' (a fundamental objective of the government White Paper *Working for Patients*),[1] there needs to be a way of defining health care in terms of cost and resources (casemix) to a level of detail which has not been available in the past. Hence health care resource groups (HRGs) have been developed to define casemix for English health care practice.

Clinical coding

A good starting point for determining cost is to relate it to diagnosis and/or treatment, especially as these data have, for decades, been routinely collected and coded using the International Classification of Disease (ICD) for diagnosis (Box 6.1) and the Office of Population Census and Surveys 'System' (OPCS) for procedures (Box 6.2). However, this process was largely for demographic study and not for the measurement of work-load or cost; consequently, although mandatory, it has been given a low clinical priority. Trained coders have been employed by all hospitals, but they have usually been divorced from the clinical setting, relying upon information provided by clinicians who often neither used the coded data nor understood the reason for their collection. Therefore, the accuracy of clinical coding to date is questionable.

Box 6.1: International Classification of Diseases, tenth revision (ICD-10)

The International Classification of Disease has its origins at the end of the eighteenth century when the *International Classification of Causes of Death* was sponsored by the International Statistical Institute. In 1929 the fourth revision was produced in collaboration with the Health Organization of the League of Nations, and by the sixth revision (1948) the World Health Organization had assumed responsibility. This revision also included for the first time 'causes of morbidity', moving away from the concept of pure mortality statistics. The ninth revision (ICD-9) was used until April 1995 and, with its limitations (see below), was the basis for the early work on HRG development. The lack of specificity seen in the example below hampered the development of more specific grouping, but this will hopefully be rectified at least in part by ICD-10, which is amply demonstrated by the codes for subarachnoid haemorrhage:

ICD 9   Subarachnoid haemorrhage   430
Meningeal haemorrhage
Ruptured (congenital) cerebral aneurysm:
    NOS (not otherwise specified)
    syphilitic

ICD 10   Subarachnoid haemorrhage   160
I60.0 Subarachnoid haemorrhage from carotid syphon and bifurcation
I60.1 Subarachnoid haemorrhage from middle cerebral artery
I60.2 Subarachnoid haemorrhage from anterior communicating artery
I60.3 Subarachnoid haemorrhage from posterior communicating artery
I60.4 Subarachnoid haemorrhage from basilar artery
I60.5 Subarachnoid haemorrhage from vertebral artery
I60.6 Subarachnoid haemorrhage from other intracranial arteries
I60.7 Subarachnoid haemorrhage from intracranial artery unspecified
I60.8 Other subarachnoid haemorrhage
I60.9 Subarachnoid haemorrhage unspecified

The codes in ICD-10 are arranged alphanumerically in 21 chapters. The first character (a letter) gives the chapter, and the next two numbers give the broad category of disease. The qualifiers 0–9 (fourth character) give greater specificity. For example:

Box 6.1: *continued*

VIII   Diseases of the ear and mastoid process (H60–H95)
H60–H62 Diseases of external ear
H63–H75 Diseases of middle ear and mastoid
H80–H83 Diseases of inner ear
H90–H95 Other disorders of ear

Diseases of the inner ear contains:

H80 Otosclerosis
H81 Disorders of vestibular function
H82 Vertiginous syndromes in diseases classified elsewhere
H83 Other diseases of inner ear

Disorders of vestibular function is further broken down into:

H81.0 Menières disease
H81.1 Benign paroxysmal vertigo
H81.2 Vestibular neuronitis
etc.

The number 9 in the fourth position is reserved for 'unspecified' conditions, as for example in H81.9 Disorders of vestibular function, unspecified.

Chapter XX (V01–Y98) is 'External causes of morbidity and mortality', which 'permits the classification of environmental events and circumstances as the cause of injury, poisoning and other adverse effects'. For example transport accidents are coded V01–V99; a pedestrian hit by a bus would be coded V04 and V95.4 is a 'Spacecraft accident injuring occupant'!

Of course, not all hospital 'episodes' are for disease, and the many variations are covered by 'V' codes. Examples of such codes are: contact with a communicable disease (tuberculosis contact V01.1), healthy live birth (V30) and screening (screening for hypertension V81.1).

Box 6.2: OPCS Classification for Surgical Operations, fourth revision

The Office of Population Census and Surveys Classification of Surgical Operations, fourth revision, was first issued in 1987, since when there have been a number of updates. Procedures are given an alphanumerical code and grouped in 23 anatomically based chapters. For example:

A   Nervous system
B   Endocrine system and breast
C   Eye

Within each chapter specific procedures are listed under broad anatomical headings, for example:

B   Endocrine system and breast

   Pituitary and pineal glands (B01–B06)
      B01 Excision of pituitary gland
      B02 Destruction of pituitary gland
      B03 Other operation on pituitary gland
      B06 Operations on pineal gland
   Thyroid and parathyroid glands (B08–B16)
   Other endocrine glands (B18–B25)
   Breast (B27–B37)

In addition to the main procedure codes, enhancements are available within Chapters Y and Z. Y codes define methods of operation, for example:

Y48   Approach to spine through back
      Y48.1 Laminectomy approach to cervical spine
      Y48.2 Laminectomy approach to thoracic spine
      Y48.3 Laminectomy approach to lumbar spine
      etc.

Z codes provide greater anatomical detail and are essential in orthopaedic surgery, for example:

Z09   Peripheral nerve of arm
      Z09.1 Circumflex nerve
      Z09.2 Median nerve
      Z09.3 Radial nerve
      etc.

Isoresource groups and the currency of contracting

Whilst it is reasonable to assume a correlation between diagnosis, procedure and the cost of a treatment 'episode', the detail of the relationship was unknown; this precluded any sophisticated contract design in the early days of the purchaser–provider split. To enable contracting to evolve, a system for the measurement of casemix needed to be developed, but the lack of detailed information regarding cost and resource use meant that assumptions had to be made; length of stay has been widely used as a proxy for resource use, and costs derived accordingly.

To develop more sophisticated contracts, individual treatment episodes need to be categorized (and coded) to reflect cost and resource use as effortlessly as possible to keep down administration costs. One system gaining popularity internationally is the concept that there are different treatment profiles that consume broadly similar resources even though they may apply to different clinical conditions; aggregations of such profiles form 'isoresource groups'.

This approach was adopted in the USA in the 1970s, when the government was concerned at the escalating costs of Medicare patients. 'Diagnosis related groups' (DRGs) were developed, in which diagnosis and/or procedure codes are used to define treatment profiles and length of stay is used as a proxy for resource use. The need for clinical relevance to the classification was recognized, and 23 'major diagnostic categories' (MDCs) were defined, to which 475 DRGs were appropriately assigned. For example:

- MDC 1: Diseases and Disorders of the Nervous System

- MDC 2: Disorders and Diseases of the Eye

- MDC 3: Diseases and Disorders of the Ear, Nose and Throat.

The diagnoses or procedures within a DRG are clinically similar.

With the advent of resource management initiative (Chapter 2), the need for a system of isoresource groupings for the NHS was recognized. Initially the expressed intention was to facilitate local resource management but it was obvious even then that a successful system could produce an ideal 'currency' for the contracting process.

In 1990 the National Casemix Office (NCMO), an arm of the NHS Management Executive (NHS) Information Management Group (IMG) established clinician-led specialty working groups with the aim of developing a UK system of isoresource groups. Early examination of the US system

showed that DRGs could not be applied unmodified to UK hospital practice,
and consequently HRGs were developed. In some specialties HRGs were
very similar to DRGs, but in other areas a completely new grouping system

---

Box 6.3: Health care resource groups, version 2

Chapter headings:
a) Nervous System
      *a01 Intracranial procedures (except trauma) w cc
      *a02 Intracranial procedures (except trauma) w/o cc
        Hemispherectomy   (OPCS code A011)
        Total lobectomy of brain   (OPCS code A012)
        Partial lobectomy of brain (OPCS code A013)
        etc.
      *a23 Viral meningitis
        Enteroviral meningitis   (ICD 10 code A870)
        Adenoviral meningitis   (ICD 10 code A871)
        Lymphocytic choriomeningitis (ICD 10 code A872)
        etc.
b) Eyes and periorbita
c) Head, neck and mouth
d) Respiratory system
e) Cardiovascular system
f) Digestive system
g) Hepatobiliary and pancreatic system
h) Musculoskeletal system
j) Skin (including burns)
k) Endocrine and metabolic
l) Urinary tract and male reproductive system
m) Female reproductive system
n) Obstetrics and gynaecology
p) Diseases of childhood
s) Poisoning, infectious diseases and non-specific groupings
t) Psychiatry
u) Undefined groups

*a01 and a02 are 'procedure driven' and hence are categorized by
OPCS codes, whereas a23 does not involve surgery and hence is
categorized by ICD10 code.

was developed. In the same way that DRGs are organized in MDCs, HRGs are arranged in chapters according to body system (for example nervous, respiratory and digestive; Box 6.3) or where more appropriate by specialty (for example diseases of childhood or psychiatry).

It was clear from the outset that HRGs would only work if they could be derived from data that were already routinely collected. It is a requirement for all inpatient episodes to be coded for ICD (Box 6.1) and, where a procedure is performed, for OPCS (Box 6.2); hence ICD9 and later (after April 1995) ICD10 and OPCS4 codes formed the basis of HRG definition, with, in some instances, other routine information such as age. Special 'grouper' software has been produced to derive HRGs automatically from these data. In the absence of information concerning resource consumption, and similar to the development of DRGs, length of stay was used as a proxy for resource use. This assumption will need to be tested in the future and HRGs modified as better costed data become available.

Obviously other factors beyond primary diagnosis and procedure have an impact on resource consumption, the most significant being complications, and co-morbidities. In those groups where these have been shown to impact significantly on length of stay, two HRGs are assigned, one with and one without complications. For example, in Version 2:

HRG description

a03 Intracranial Procedures for Trauma w cc

a04 Intracranial Procedures for Trauma w/o cc

(w cc = with complications or co-morbidity; w/o cc = without complications or co-morbidity).

Note: by convention, the group consuming the *greater* resources (a03) has the *lower* numeric value.

Age is also a significant determinant of resource consumption in some conditions and where this is the case, two HRGs are again used. For example:

HRG description

a17 Non-transient Stroke/Cerebrovascular Accident > 59 years

a18 Non-transient Stroke/Cerebrovascular Accident < 60 years.

It is anticipated that the greater specificity of Read Codes will facilitate further refinement of HRGs.

Because of the different central administration of the NHS in Scotland, Wales and Northern Ireland, the system has only been in the first instance applied to England. Wales has opted to use DRGs, and Northern Ireland and Scotland are in the process of selecting a system.

One consequence of using ICD and OPCS codes to derive HRGs has been to raise the profile of clinical coding to improve the accuracy. Errors can lead to assignment of the wrong contract group, with potential financial implications; incomplete information, such as failure to record an operation, will lead to HRG assignment on the basis of diagnosis alone and usually to a lower priced contract group. Failure to record secondary diagnoses, such as deep vein thrombosis and chest infection (examples of complications), or diabetes mellitus and rheumatoid arthritis (examples of co-morbidities), can 'downgrade' a contract group, again with implications for reimbursement.

Contract types

Lack of accurate and appropriate data meant that contracts were initially very simple, but more sophisticated models are slowly evolving. Block contracts, many of which are still in use, were the first models used. In its simplest form the block contract merely specifies a number of patient 'treatments' (finished consultant episodes: FCEs) for a fixed sum of money and may encompass the entire range of treatments offered by a hospital trust (provider unit) to a purchaser. Hence overperformance in one clinical area or 'directorate' may balance underperformance in another. With this model purchasers are relatively protected because they are 'immune' to changes in complexity and can accurately predict expenditure for the period of the contract (usually one year). In some ways the corporate management of provider units is also protected, in that income is guaranteed if the appropriate number of FCEs is achieved. However at a directorate level there is potentially a greater risk, especially as few hospitals have developed sophisticated internal trading, whereby money is transferred between services in proportion to work-load. Consequently a directorate may treat more patients or treat a more complex spectrum of patients without any financial compensation, with the end result of being unable to stay within budget. Similarly another directorate may underperform without financial penalty. For this reason simple block contracts are no longer allowed by the NHSE.

Certain purchasers, particularly GP fundholders, and some providers are pushing for the development of more specific contracts. These take two basic form: cost and volume, and cost per case. 'Cost and volume' is a variance on block contracts, whereby a core level of work-load is guaranteed to be purchased at a price; activity beyond that guaranteed level is purchased by mutual agreement but at a lower unit price. This recognizes that treating an extra patient only incurs 'marginal' costs, since the costs of the hospital's infrastructure have already been recovered in the core contract. Cost and volume contracts also usually include 'penalties' for underperformance by the provider.

'Cost per case' contracts offer no guarantees to the provider; a full cost is agreed for types of treatment and that price is paid for every patient treated. At first sight, these contracts may seem attractive to providers, but work-load, and therefore income, is unpredictable, making them particularly risky in financial terms. However, agreed prices usually distinguish between treatments, and the money truly follows the patient, i.e. the more work done, the more money earned, although equally, less work yields less income.

'Casemix, cost and volume' contracts are a compromise between cost and volume and cost per case contracts. Not only does the contract specify the number of cases treated, but also the spectrum of complexity (casemix) is recognized for its impact upon resource consumption. To this end HRGs are a valuable means of specifying the variability in resource use. This is clearly a potentially fairer system than the average specialty cost applied in cost and volume contracts, but to be worth the additional administrative costs, there probably has to be a broad range of complexity within the service and the potential for casemix to change year on year. In general surgery, for example, it would be worth considering for vascular surgery (high cost, low volume), but, for a service made up of predictably large volumes of herniorrhaphies, gall bladder and varicose vein surgery with few of the major abdominal procedures, the transaction costs may be hard to justify.

Pricing of contracts

Whilst guidance on currencies for contracting is still emerging, guidance on costing abounds and is currently being refined.

Unlike the private sector the current rules of the internal market emphasize that price must equal cost, i.e. no 'profit' or cross-subsidization between treatment types is allowed.

However, some flexibility in this assumption may be introduced in subsequent contracting negotiations, i.e. for certain procedures, price will be what the market can bear. Even so certain purchasers will continue to demand that costing details are provided to support the prices charged for treatments, so costing methods must be rigorous.

Setting a price involves two basic stages: top-down cost allocation and bottom-up treatment resource profiling.

The objective of top-down cost allocation is to push costs down to the level for which contracts are signed. In a hospital most contracts, and consequently most income, are for clinical services; therefore those clinical services have to recover in their prices the full cost of the hospital rather than simply their own direct costs.

Top-down cost allocation is a well-established process whereby overhead or central costs, such as for estates services, general management, finance and personnel, are apportioned over the clinical support and direct patient care departments, usually on the basis of 'static' reference data such as floor area or head count. The clinical support departments for example pathology and radiology, are in turn then apportioned to each directorate on the basis of use and added to the costs of wards and theatres to establish the directorates' total costs.

The result of this process is to absorb the whole cost of the hospital into the clinical directorates. The impact is that while the direct costs of a directorate may be £1 million, its fully absorbed costs may be £2 million or even £3 million.

The means by which costs are apportioned to directorates is a matter for some debate, since accurate usage data are not always readily available, particularly for high-volume services such as pathology. The validity of proxy measures is at best often questionable. Whatever the doubts over methodology, the full cost of each directorate represents the amount that must be recovered by price, given an assumed number of patients treated.

The relative prices of treatments within a directorate are established through bottom-up costing. This should heavily involve clinical staff in defining broad care profiles for each treatment. The profiles incorporating length of stay, nursing dependency, theatres and other key resources should concentrate on the major elements of cost rather than on what may be clinically significant but of low cost.

Once all treatments have an agreed profile for costing, these are used as weights applied to the planned numbers of patients to absorb the full cost of the directorate.

In the example in Table 6.1, 'cost units' for each profile item have been used to build up the total weight. Cost units in this context are the costs of a day in bed or an hour in theatre, calculated as part of the top-down costing process. If the theatre's fully absorbed cost is £250 000 per annum, with a

Table 6.1: This shows how, using bottom-up resource profiling, the fully absorbed cost of a directorate (in this case £1 000 000) is absorbed into different treatments based on their relative weights (RVUs). The approach guarantees the full recovery of costs through prices given expected activity levels (volume)

Profile	Treatment A			Treatment B		Treatment C	
	Volume	Cost units	Total	Volume	Total	Volume	Total
Length of stay	5 days	100	500	3	300	1	100
Theatre	1 hour	200	200	0.5	0	5	100
Nursing	10	150	1500	6	900	4	600
Total weight			2200		1200		800
No. of cases			300		50		100
Weight × no. of cases			660 000		60 000		80 000

The weights × volumes produces what are known as relative value units (RVUs)

Total RVUs for the directorate (660 000 + 60 000 + 80 000) = 800 000

Therefore the actual cost of a RVU is $\dfrac{1\,000\,000}{800\,000}$ = £1.25

Therefore the prices for A–C are:

	Weight	RVU cost	Price (£)	Volume	Total income (£)
A	2200	1.25	2750	300	825 000
B	1200	1.25	1500	50	75 000
C	800	1.25	1000	100	100 000

planned utilization of 2000 hours, the cost unit would be £125 per hour. They exclude any costs specifically identified as another separate item in the profile.

For instance in the example given, the length of stay cost unit would cover all costs related to a day as an inpatient, except that of nursing, since nursing is separately identified as part of the profile.

Using profiles for relative weighting, rather than to set an absolute price, avoids the risk that incomplete or wrong profiles will not recover the full cost of the directorate. Experience suggests that while top-down costing is fairly robust, bottom-up profiling requires further development. Clinical input into bottom-up costing must be increased since, if the 'currency' has no clinical significance, it is not possible to establish meaningful profiles or accurate costs.

Notwithstanding such specific clinical input, increasing comfort with HRGs has resulted in the NHSE requiring trusts to cost HRGs in up to six specialties during the year 1995/96. Such a move suggests that, whatever local contracting 'currencies' may be negotiated, HRG costs are likely to be used for national comparisons and 'benchmarking'.

Conclusion

In conclusion a whole new science is upon us in health care delivery, founded upon the principle that the 'money should follow the patient'. It begins with the accurate recording of clinical data, leading to quality coding and an understanding of the relevant costs and resource implications. This information underpins contract negotiations between the 'purchaser' and 'provider' of health care and should ensure appropriate reimbursement for those who do the work. Of course participants in the 'market' must not lose sight of the fact that other issues, such as efficiency, quality and outcome, although outside the scope of this article, are paramount in the procurement of health care.

Reference

1   Department of Health (1989) *Working for Patients* (Cmnd 555). HMSO, London.

7 Shared care or integrated care? Managing clinical services for chronic disease across the interfaces

Bob Young

Rationale

The principal objective of any health care service is to achieve the best possible levels of personal service and clinical outcome, both individually and collectively, within the available resources. Traditionally health care professionals have tended to work as individuals doing the best, as they saw it, for individual patients. This is increasingly recognized as inappropriate and inefficient; teamwork often delivers better care. However the teams needed to carry out a heart transplant or manage a prostatectomy is very different from those needed for diabetes care, asthma, rheumatoid arthritis or inflammatory bowel disease, for example, in which the necessary personnel are both multidisciplinary and distributed between primary and secondary health care sectors and between specialist sectors. This chapter describes some arrangements that are proving valuable in managing such services and which extend teamwork across traditional organizational and professional boundaries towards the concept of integrated care rather than simple sharing between functionally unaltered units.

The messages of this chapter have been deduced from the context of a diabetes care service. Potentially, however, the principles could apply equally to the management of almost any chronic disease, for example, asthma, hypertension, psoriasis, rheumatoid arthritis, depression, schizophrenia, many cancers or inflammatory bowel disease. All of these conditions are characterized by being:

- relatively common

- susceptible to timely appropriate interventions

- often managed by fragmented and uncoordinated services

- relatively expensive to the health service (e.g. diabetes alone accounts for at least 5% of NHS spending).

It is also generally recognized that no one sector of the health service can or should manage these conditions exclusively. There is a need for parallel access to different 'strata' of care rather than the more conventional model of stepwise exchange between care levels. Typically among any population of patients with a particular chronic disorder:

- all will require primary care services
- many will, at some time, require specialized secondary care services
- some will require highly specialized secondary care services
- a few will require highly specialized tertiary level services.

Thus blindness due to diabetic retinopathy, hitherto the most common cause of new blindness in people of working age, is now largely preventable and a good example to consider. To achieve optimum outcome for a population of patients with diabetes, all patients require optimization of glycaemic control and regular retinal screening. Many patients will at some time require diabetes centre advice for education, improvement of metabolic control or evaluation of developing retinopathy. Some patients will require argon laser retinal photocoagulation for sight-threatening retinopathy, and a few may need vitreoretinal surgery. Patients with diabetes want to be confident that their needs will be accurately ascertained and that they will achieve access, without fuss, to the appropriate level of service at each stage in their life with diabetes. They do not wish to encounter delays, barriers or inflexibilities at any of the interfaces. They will also wish to be reassured that these different elements of service (which represent only a small part of the totality of diabetes care) can integrate effectively in a manner that will indeed ensure the prevention of blindness.

The team players

The various 'players' in the complex distributed team responsible for delivering chronic disease management will inevitably view their parts from different perspectives. Indeed it is quite likely that they will, at the outset, not even appreciate that they are part of a wider disease management 'team'.

Fusing these perceptions into an integrated vision is the essential art of ensuring that comprehensive, accessible, effective and efficient chronic disease services are provided within NHS resources.

The patient

The patient is a player in his or her own right in chronic disease treatment. Whereas individuals can be almost totally passive and achieve a good outcome if they have pneumonia, an inguinal hernia, cataract or even an organ transplant, the success or failure of chronic disease treatment depends crucially on the patients' contributions. This requires that they be motivated and have the necessary knowledge, and that their individual life circumstances are taken into account within agreed management plans. So whereas there are collective goals, these are contingent upon meeting effectively the needs of multiple individuals.

The primary health care team

The primary health care team will deal with every patient but has many other simultaneous demands and pressures. With respect to any particular chronic disease it needs to know precisely what its responsibilities are within the broader picture and to understand the boundaries of its expertise. It must have a clear view of the overall expectations or treatment goals for groups of people with chronic disease and not set its sights too low. To this end it requires clear guidance on the thresholds for referral that will be beneficial. Primary health care teams will also wish to be reassured that patients do not become inappropriately 'trapped' in a secondary or tertiary care level of the network. There can clearly be a tension between providing a first-rate primary care level chronic disease management service and overconfidence in practice level resources, particularly if there appear to be disincentives to referral (rural practices, poor perceptions of secondary care services, inappropriately low expectations of good outcome or GP fundholding); this can be a problem when the incidence of major adverse outcomes within individual general practices is low.

Secondary care services

Secondary care services cannot adopt the isolated 'prima donna' specialist posture in chronic disease management. To complement the other parts of the service, they must organize in such a way that they provide a responsive and clearly communicative service that discharges its roles comprehensively. These roles must meet the perceived needs of patients and GPs. This means, for example, elimination of unnecessary duplication, agreeing thresholds for referral, responding promptly when requested, and providing clear guidance for ongoing management rather than assuming total responsibility.

More specialist services

More specialist secondary and tertiary level services also need to develop a sensible appreciation of their role in the overall care process, focusing attention on providing that part of the service for which only they have the skills. In turn they must link, in a structured way, to the referring services such that they provide a responsive and appropriate service.

The purchaser

The purchaser or commissioner of services can easily be bewildered by this sort of scenario. Hopefully, he will recognize his responsibility for ensuring that the people within his area have a service that is meeting their needs, both immediately, in service level structure and process terms, and in the long-term, with regard to delivering effective health care and minimizing adverse outcomes. How is the purchaser/commissioner going to contract for a service that, clearly, can be delivered only by a large variety of interacting services, some of which will always be in primary care, some of which may be in the community sector, some of which can be delivered by local NHS Trust(s) and some of which may have to be delivered by a more distant regional centre? Probably, for major chronic diseases, it will be necessary to devise, if it does not already exist, some sort of disease or condition-specific organizational structure that transcends the traditional, and otherwise often quite appropriate, organizational boundaries of NHS provider organizations in respect of delivering agreed standards of service and outcomes for those particular conditions. The alternative scenario, which would involve purchasers/commissioners in trying to negotiate independently with all the contributory parties, leads inevitably to nightmarish complexity and a degree of engagement by purchasers in provider management decisions for which they have neither the resources nor the expertise. Much better, I believe, is to try and set up, as it were, consortia of primary secondary and tertiary care providers who can in collaboration provide a comprehensive service, and to operate through some agreed and accountable managerial structure in which the purchaser/commissioner can negotiate. How could this be done in practice?

Approach

Locality-based condition-specific management organizations

In recognition of the issues outlined in the proceeding section, locality-based provider groups are already emerging. Local diabetes services advisory groups are an example. Typically they comprise:

- primary care nominees (e.g. the local medical committee, the medical audit advisory group and the practice nurse)

- diabetes centre nominees (physicans, diabetes specialist nurse, dietitian, chiropodist, pathology staff and paediatrician)

- community nominees (community dietetic and community chiropody staff, and optometrists)

- patient representatives

- commissioner nominees (director of public health or manager)

- specialist nominees as required (e.g. from ophthalmology, nephrology, obstetrics and gynaecology or vascular surgery).

It is now clear from experience around the country that such groups are able to debate and agree local policy. Some have progressed to the point of managing the necessary changes in local service provision and setting and monitoring standards of care. The logical next step, it seems to me, is to make the chairman and an executive subgroup of such bodies budget holders for diabetes care services and thus accountable for the services provided. I think that the person most appropriate to take on such a role is a consultant physician with a special interest in diabetes, the same being true for most other chronic disease, since such people have the best perspective for the services as a whole and should always be fully aware of the most up-to-date effective health care measures in their area of special interest. Such people, however, must be prepared, and able, to work in a collaborative culture.

Guidelines

Guidelines have a crucial role to play in the management of such services in the future. They can provide a framework within which such a disparate group of providers is able to deliver a coherent service. Such guidelines need to be 'minimalist', in the sense that they define only the essential irreducible standards necessary to optimize outcome, yet retain enough 'space' to allow individual health care providers to work innovatively and sensitively. Such guidelines will consider in detail only key processes and be predominantly outcome-oriented. They will usually need to cover:

- when and how to carry out key processes
- when and how to communicate, document, etc.
- the definition of roles and responsibilities
- standards of responsiveness
- thresholds for referral, discharge, etc.

Needless to say such guidelines must be framed within the context of an overall statement of aims and objectives. It is the responsibility of the locality services group to define these objectives, and it should be increasingly possible to do so in terms of patient benefits. If all providers agree on these objectives, appropriate guidelines in respect of the different providers' responsibilities and the ways in which they should interact can be negotiated according to local circumstances. The guidelines then both define the tasks that have to be managed and create an audit trail against which service effectiveness can be tested.

Thus, to take an example once again from diabetes care services, there is the important objective of minimizing the number of amputations. Here the different parts of the network might operate in the following way.

- Primary care services have the roles of:
    - minimizing the development of neuropathy and peripheral vascular disease through advice on risk behaviours (e.g. smoking), obtaining and maintaining good glycaemic, blood pressure and lipid control, and referring on to the diabetes centre patients failing to meet therapeutic targets
    - identifying patients with asymptomatic peripheral neuropathy or peripheral vascular disease and referring on to community chiropody services for intensified preventative foot care/education

- Community chiropody services:
    - deliver intensified preventive foot care of 'at risk' feet and treatment of minor lesions
    - identify and refer major lesions without delay

- Diabetes centre (high-risk foot clinic):
  - manages high-risk foot lesions, admitting patients when necessary
  - delivers a broad package of metabolic and physical (orthotic/customized footwear) measures for long-term prevention
  - identifies those patients who need vascular reconstruction/amputation

- Vascular surgical services:
  - carry out vascular reconstruction and timely minimized amputations when necessary

- Rehabilitation services:
  - provide prostheses and collaborate in secondary prevention of disease in the remaining limb.

It can be seen from this that each of these areas will need to develop guidelines for internal multidisciplinary working within them, thresholds for referral/discharge and standards of communication. As is now well-recognized, however, such guidelines will prove worthless unless there is some form of monitoring to assess the consistency with which they are applied.

Monitoring and control

The sort of service model being described is predicated on the ability to monitor the associated contracts or quality performance. It is inconceivable that this could be achieved without some sort of dedicated information system. Furthermore all the participants need relevant feedback. Accordingly an information system appropriate to a locality chronic disease service requires that:

- individual patients:
  - understand their role and the services that are available to them

- practices know:
  - how many patients they have with the condition concerned
  - whether the processes for which they are responsible are up-to-date
  - how they are performing compared with their peers
  - whether they are being renumerated for their work

- hospital services know:
  - activity levels subdivided into major problem areas and sources
  - administrative performance, particularly in relation to communication
  - process performance, for example achievement of key process measures such as retinopathy screening
  - intermediate and endpoint outcome performance
  - casemix-adjusted performance in comparison with similar services

- locality groups managing the services know:
  - performance against standards set by service and by provider
  - achievement rates compared with comparable benchmarked services
  - costs in relation to achievements

- the commissioner/purchaser knows:
  - performance against contract in terms of activity and quality.

There are no NHS information systems that can at present supply such information. Various forms of condition-specific, locality-based information system have been successfully devised and implemented. In common with all other information systems, it is ideal if the system itself can both assist the pro-viders in carrying their tasks and simultaneously gather necessary quality and management information. In this area of delivering effective, evidence-based medicine for chronic diseases, there is a strong case for constructive and imaginative integration of primary care medical audit advisory groups and Trust clinical audit boards with locality condition-specific management groups. There will usually be a need for an individual to take primary re-sponsibility for data gathering, information production and use, and such a person is likely to play a key role in the condition-specific locality manage-ment group.

The management of change

For most localities the concept of organizing integrated services itself represents a major change. As soon as the roles and responsibilities become explicit and people start understanding, through appropriate information systems, exactly what they are doing rather than what they have perceived themselves to be doing, further major changes become inevitable. The nature of medical progress and continuous change in health service organization, along with an intrinsic tendency for complex organizations to degenerate, means that managing change is a continuous and indefinite process. The locality condition-specific management group must therefore devise appro-priate mechanisms for enabling this to happen. Although managers of individual services, from practice level upwards, will each play an important part, the role of service leader (probably a consultant from a locality hospital as suggested above) is crucial. Such a person must:

- ensure that purchasers, providers and patients are all aware of what can and ought to be achieved

- build up trust and respect throughout the diverse but integrated provider network

- ensure that each part of the network, which will also have responsibilities for many other demands, understands its role in the delivery of this particular chronic disease management programme and accepts its responsibility to perform to defined and monitorable standards

- negotiate, persuade, cajole, lead and see though real changes in the structure, process and outcome of service delivery, according to realistic timescales

- accept the responsibility and accountability for providing a service in which his or her own professional skills are only one, albeit important, part of the jigsaw.

This is a major management task, which considerably extends the standard role of the consultant physician. It goes without saying that a willingness and ability to work with others in teams, and to lead diverse and distributed groups of multiprofessional health care providers, are essential attributes that go well beyond most senior registrars' training. This will clearly have to change. Appropriate courses are already available for consultants and senior registrars. There seems little doubt that contracts and job specifications will gradually adapt to the new reality.

The integrated care service

This chapter has argued that integrated care is a logical and appropriate way to approach the management of chronic diseases. Establishing such services entails major organizational changes. The scale of these should not be underestimated, but the potential rewards in terms of service effectiveness are enormous. From my own experience a number of factors are prerequisites of success. These include:

- building up trust between providers who have deep historical mutual suspicions; there must be willingness to consider things from the other party's standpoint, to acknowledge past failures and to demonstrate good faith with appropriate actions

- team building at all levels; so often this is based on building up personal links, mutual respect, role definition and shared goals

- clear leadership, including realistic and appropriate goal definitions, firmness of purpose, adjustment of resource allocation where necessary and a willingness to acknowledge that success will often be achieved vicariously

- fairness, including a commitment from the outset to share and improve rather than to shift or dismiss (dump or decline)

- patience.

I believe that integrated care services for chronic diseases will become the norm within the next ten years. I do not envisage that there will be a uniform model because there will inevitably have to be adaptation to the circumstances of each locality. That such services will be required to perform to explicitly monitored standards of both process and outcome, and will be lead by specialists with a locality-wide management role, seem likely to be consistent features. The benefits should be higher standards of service delivery and outcome that are much more unified and consistent than at present.

8 Managing quality through outcome measurement and audit

Sue Lydeard and Steve George

In the short time since writing the first draft of this chapter, the winds of change have once again blown through quality management and rendered obsolete the terminology, although not, we are pleased to say, the underlying issue. So where we originally extolled the virtues of medical then clinical audit, clinical outcomes then effectiveness, we now find that it is really all about evidence-based practice, and a little bird tells us that perhaps we should actually be writing about managed care.

Of course this is pure semantics because it is all the same thing. Managing quality is about agreeing and meeting the customer's requirements with the minimum of resource use; that applies whether the customer is the commissioner of the service, the beneficiary of the service or the payer for the service. No matter what the latest jargon attached to the tools of the trade, quality in health care is *managed by measuring it*.

In the absence of good, hard measures of performance against attributes and characteristics of our service that are important enough to identify and specify, we will not know what quality of service we are delivering and how it compares to recognized 'best practice' in a clinical sense or against standards of service agreed in contracts.

For ease of understanding and management, 'quality' is best considered as an issue of either service delivery or clinical quality. The former is associated with the Patient's Charter[1] and contract standards, such as waiting times and GP communications, whilst the latter is concerned with diagnosis, treatment and care (Figures 8.1 and 8.2). Specifying, measuring and managing the quality of service delivery is very important; clinical quality is more difficult to evaluate and therefore forms the focus of this chapter.

The issue of defining, measuring, monitoring and improving clinical quality is paramount, because whether you look at clinical practice among practitioners, hospitals, regions or countries, the variations are enormous, even when allowances are made for age, sex and other variables. Patients with similar characteristics who present to different clinicians get different treatments, and the principal cause of these differences is that doctors do not agree about what is 'best practice'. Pilot studies by the World Health

SERVICE DELIVERY	CLINICAL QUALITY
Patient's Charter	Clinical guidelines
Contract standards	Evidence-based practice
Service specification	Managed care
Relatively easy	Difficult
Top-down	Bottom-up
Aggregated data	Individual patient focus
Relative consistency	Huge variation

Figure 8.1: Specifying quality.

Organization have shown that these differences cannot be blamed on lack of resources, poor professional skill or low professional ethics.[2] The cause is a lack of awareness that these differences are occurring. In addition health professionals are not motivated to evaluate their work or improve it. They need mechanisms to help them to monitor the services they provide and to ensure their quality.

So what is clinical quality?

The medical profession has, traditionally, been reluctant to define clinical quality, claiming that it is an elusive concept, whilst the public and individual

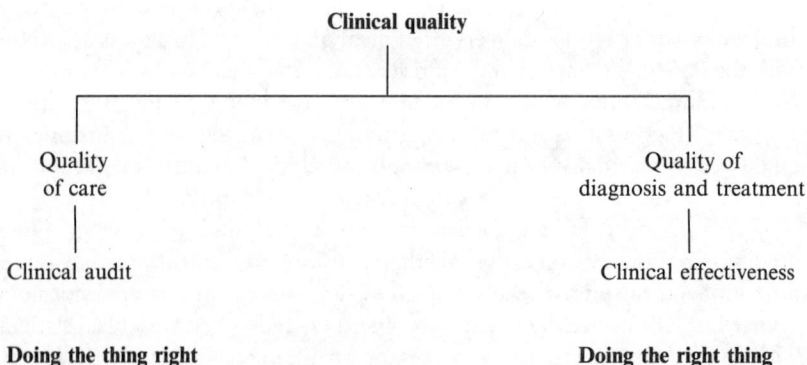

Figure 8.2: Measurement of performance.

consumers assume that there is a high quality of care; they do not consciously think that their care may in a clinical sense be inadequate. By definition 'best practice' will achieve the best outcome, but the problems arise because 'best practice' may not be measured (or even measurable); if it is the information may not be widely disseminated. Furthermore it may not be 'owned' and therefore may not be accepted as best practice.

Caper[3] has defined the three components of quality as efficacy, appropriateness and the caring function of medicine. Efficacy is the concern that a diagnostic or therapeutic procedure accomplishes its goal. Although a particular diagnostic or therapeutic course of action may be appropriate in some circumstances, the costs, risks and benefits must be assessed in each case. The caring function of medicine involves the interpersonal, supportive and psychological aspects of the professional–patient relationship.

More recently researchers and practitioners are recognizing the importance of patient-focused care, as opposed to organization-centred care, and another definition of the quality of care could be the degree to which the outcomes desired by patients and their carers are achieved.

Quality of care

A critical part of the NHS agenda has always implicitly been to improve quality of care and obtain value for money. Since the implementation of general management and the NHS reforms, this has been made more and more explicit by introducing systems to review quality of clinical care received by patients. Valid and reliable information and supporting systems facilitate the review of clinical practice in which:

- clinical staff must be involved with the production of information and committed to its integrity

- the information must be patient-centred and clinically relevant

- quality information about clinical performance accepted by the clinicians can then be compared

- measurable differences in behaviour between clinicians do not require prescriptive action, since most clinicians are not only extremely competitive but also want to deliver best practice

- clinicians accept the need for change when the information demonstrates that they are not doing as well as they thought they were.

Much routine clinical information relates to length of stay of the patients and the resources used during the episode, for example investigations, theatre time and drugs. It is therefore possible to discuss with colleagues the relevance, effectiveness and appropriateness of these interventions for individual patients, and how the outcomes compare with others, and make recommendations for future improvements. It is also possible to group patients together according to a number of different parameters and compare not only the outcomes achieved but also the resource implications for achieving them.

Information about an individual's performance can be perceived as threatening, and this has to be handled with tact and sensitivity; however the more that information is shared, the easier this will be. It is the use of this type of information that may help to explain the wide variations that exist between individual clinicians, hospitals and health districts. Development and ownership of guidelines or standards of accepted best practice does, however, create a dual responsibility; the clinician must be prepared to change but equally must be allowed the resources to do so by those who share the information. Mishandling this scenario will result in resistance and unnecessary disharmony.

Quality of diagnosis/treatment

One aspect of clinical information that is still lagging behind is the measurement of clinical effectiveness, what happens to the patient as a result of the health care intervention? Activity, casemix, procedures and cost have, until now, been the focus of attention, and part of the reason for apparent reluctance to venture into measuring effectiveness is because it is so complex. The immediate benefit of measuring effectiveness is, on the one hand, getting it right for the patient and, on the other, using the routinely collected information to develop profiles of care against which performance can be monitored. Quantifying the process is important in terms of what you do, how much it costs and how many people you do it to, but it is incomplete information for management purposes unless there is some means of identifying what actually happened to the patient and therefore the quality of treatment provided.

Outcome indicators

There is widespread interest in developing outcome indicators that reflect quality of health care, and many of the new indicators measure the outcome of diagnosis and treatment rather than the process of care. The power of these to identify good practice has been used to good effect by the World Health Organization in areas such as the management of diabetes, the prevention of surgical wound infections and oral health care to reduce dental caries.[2] For example infections from surgical wounds have been cut by 25–50% in some hospitals in Denmark and Italy, saving bed days and enormous costs. Five years ago only a few surgical departments in Denmark performed this kind of self-evaluation because surgeons resisted the activity. Over the last few years, however, the importance of evaluation has been accepted, and now nearly 80% of all surgical departments in Denmark actively monitor the process and outcome of care.

The idea of measuring the quality of care with outcome indicators is being explored in various new areas, such as mental illness, acute respiratory diseases, maternal and child care, cardiovascular disease including stroke, and the whole area of the care of the elderly. For instance monitoring the care of stroke patients would require:

- the outcome indicators for stroke to be chosen, by consensus, on the basis of which indicators are relevant, valid, obtainable and measure good practice in stroke care
- health professionals to collect and analyse their own data consistently, with a specially developed user-friendly information system
- comparative databases to be set up that highlight the best performing centres
- wide dissemination and promotion of successful practice.

Outcome measures: holy grail or old hat?

There is a subtle but important difference between an outcome indicator and an outcome measure. The former is a general 'signpost' that we are on the right road, whilst the latter is a much more specific landmark that can provide scientifically valid and reliable evidence of best practice. Comparing performance against outcome indicators is not the same as measuring outcomes themselves, and the ability to measure what the real results of health care interventions are must still be considered to be the ultimate test of success. The scientific and consistent achievement of these measures is, however, fraught with difficulties.

It has been estimated that fewer than 20% of medical interventions have been formally evaluated in terms of specific patient outcome measures, which are an essential prerequisite to the calculation of cost-effectiveness.[4] The pace of technological change is such that evaluators are hard pressed to keep up with new innovations and have little time to revisit long-accepted but unproven treatments and practices. In addition to new technology, drugs and medical/surgical practices, there is a sizeable proportion of the activity undertaken within a health service that does not consist of 'medical' interventions, and a smaller but still significant group of activities that would not be considered by most observers to constitute a 'clinical' intervention, whoever carried it out. Such activities include, for instance, the administration of a health service, the training of personnel, and the cleaning and maintenance of capital investments. Assessment of the effectiveness and efficiency of health services must include all of the above activities.

There are three areas of work involved in this assessment:

- the identification of appropriate outcome measures, i.e. variables in which an intervention might produce a change

- the identification and validation of methods that will reliably detect the change in a variable, which is termed an outcome

- the measurement of such changes in an unbiased manner and, using epidemiological principles, their causal attribution to the intervention being assessed.

Not surprisingly, given the pressures of time and resources, many investigators move to the third area without either addressing the first two areas themselves or capitalizing upon the results of prior workers in a field.

Questions of definition: identifying outcome variables

In terms of those activities which would be deemed clinical, most evaluation work has concentrated on activities that can be easily defined. A single operative procedure with a single easily measured outcome parameter, such as immediate survival, is the ideal subject of evaluation research. However much health service activity, and consequently expenditure, is in areas that would seem to be the exact opposite of this ideal. A profile or package of care might require many and varied inputs of a multitude of types and from a variety of sources; in a chronic condition improvement may not be expected, and the best prognosis may be only a slowing of a progressive deterioration in patient condition. Where some of the inputs to such a clinical scenario are of the non-clinical type previously referred to, the problems of measurement and attribution of effect are made doubly difficult. Even the definition of the condition or care group under study is difficult, as is often the case in mental health studies, and the complexities of study design seem almost insurmountable.

In groups such as disabled people some outcome measures will relate to the acceleration of ill health or disability (such as the development of pressure sores), the implications of which may or may not be fully appreciated by a disabled person. However health professionals may also identify objectives, such as dressing independently, that reflect, for example, their enthusiasm for the patient's achievement but which may conflict directly with the preference of the disabled person. The patient or carer may want to save time and undue physical exertion by employing an assistant for dressing and this variable anyway may or may not relate to the acceleration of ill health or disability.

Thus variables identified by professionals may in some cases be vital for a disabled person's continuing health but in others may lead to a misuse of resources in pursuing objectives that do not relate to, or are not desired by, a particular individual. Measures of the effectiveness of intervention must therefore take into account not only a professional viewpoint of the implications of the patient's impairments and the efficacy of the measures that might help to minimize their handicap, but also that disabled people receiving services are a heterogenous group, with diverse medical diagnoses and with goals and expectations that will vary between different age groups and ethnic backgrounds.

Even this may not be the end of the story; the perspective of the informal carers (often a spouse or parents) of a disabled person must also be taken into account. Some of these perspectives will relate to the carers' objectives and expectations for the disabled person, which may not be the same as those held by the disabled person themselves. Carers may also have needs of their own, for instance for respite or changes in the environment, that are in direct conflict with those of the disabled person, and these competing needs must be balanced in order to produce an optimum outcome for all concerned.

Questions of measurement: finding and validating instruments that will reliably detect changes bought about by intervention

In broad terms the outcomes of any health intervention can be measured in three areas:

- mortality

- morbidity

- subjective measures of health status.

The validity and reliability of an instrument must itself be measured and a tool chosen that is appropriate to the purpose for which it will be used. The measurement of mortality, for example, is used to determine resource allocation within the NHS. Mortality itself may not be a valid measure of need for resources, but it is a reliable measurement. At the other extreme, measures of subjective health status may be valid in assessing the average perceived health of a group under study, but their distribution through a population is such that, in terms of the health of a single individual, they may be termed unreliable.

There is a bewildering variety of measures of global, psychological and social health, and of quality of life and life satisfaction, as well as more specific measures of pain, functional disability and handicap, many of which purport to be outcome measurement instruments.

So how should an outcome measure be selected for certain situations? First of all the existing literature on measurement instruments must be searched systematically, in order to provide information on which scales exist and for what use they were intended. To avoid duplication of effort, the literature must also be searched for information showing that particular instruments can be safely discounted and are not worthy of further study. As different authors have pointed out, this still leaves a lot of measurement instruments.[5,6,7]

A central dilemma exists as to whether a single global measure should be used in all situations, thus allowing easy comparison of results obtained from studies of widely differing patient groups, or whether it would be preferable to use individual instruments that are more sensitive and specific to particular situations. In order to resolve this dilemma, it is necessary to consider the purpose of the study. If a study is intended to provide information relating to an improvement in quality of care for a single patient group, it is obviously better to use an instrument specific to that group. However if a study is intended to provide data that will allow a health purchaser to decide between the allocation of resources between different patient groups, a 'common currency' needs to be used and a global measure is more appropriate. These general measures are closer to the indicators discussed above. If possible, one should kill two birds with one stone, and use both.

Questions of attribution: the measurement of outcome variable changes in an unbiased manner and their causal attribution to the intervention being assessed

The 'gold standard' for the assessment of new clinical interventions is the randomized controlled trial. Although randomized controlled trials are in principle the best method of demonstrating scientifically that one intervention produces more or less effect than another (or a placebo), there are limitations. The design will often produce a highly artificial situation within a trial, which is not found in real life; in practice the effectiveness of an intervention on a wider group of patients than that used in a trial is essential. Many people fail to understand that 'randomized' refers to random allocation to treatment rather than to random selection from a population. It must be ensured that the full range of possible outcome variables, both beneficial and harmful, is taken into account in comparing two or more treatments. Finally the resource consequences of different treatments need to be taken into account to decide on cost-effectiveness, and, in a way analogous to the selection of outcome measures, the costs to all parties must be considered.

There will be problems associated with the evaluation of any health intervention, for example, health promotion. Evaluating such activity poses great difficulties, not least of which is the selection and validation of outcome measurements discussed earlier. In addition there are difficulties in randomization between sites. Since it is often impossible to randomize health promotion at the level of the individual, one must therefore attempt to control for confounders in other ways. It is also important to recognize that there may be diffusion of the chosen intervention to control groups, and thus to employ a pragmatic approach to the design of any evaluation.

Process measures and clinical audit: gaining the moral high ground or getting lost in the swamp

Clinical audit should be seen within the broader framework of quality assurance (QA) and is a method for assisting in delivering best practice once it has been identified, in other words for measuring quality of care. It was given impetus in 1989 as part of the NHS reforms, and millions of pounds were ring-fenced to secure the medical profession's involvement in quality assurance. This investment was necessary and outweighed that set aside for other health care professionals because the medical profession had not embraced the QA initiative as warmly as had their nursing colleagues; QA being (and in some perhaps still being) in many hospitals perceived to be a nursing issue. Medical, nursing and therapy audit are focused on the professional, whereas clinical audit focuses on the patient and as such therefore evaluates the package of care as the patient experiences it rather than how the professionals deliver it.

Attention has now turned to clinical audit, but for many clinicians their own professional audit has not yet become a routine part of clinical practice, and the shift in focus to a multidisciplinary activity at best confuses the issue and at worst gives certain laggards somewhere to hide. Audit is not a difficult process, and for this reason there are many critics who question the huge investment that has been made in its promotion, and query whether or not sufficient attention has been paid to its evaluation and hence a demonstration of value for money.

There is no doubt that the major obstacles for most professionals are time and perceived threat. The former is directly related to a perception of the activity's usefulness and the latter to whether or not it is seen as a search for best practice or bad apples. Both affect the worth of audit as a tool for change and continuous quality improvement, as it is relatively easy to pay lip service to the activity by choosing a topic that can be either relatively trivial, geared to support a research interest or simply a self-congratulatory exercise. It requires commitment to the need to measure clinical effectiveness in terms of whether an intervention was the correct one, at the correct time and conducted correctly, and courage to learn from meaningful comparisons with colleagues. It also requires an understanding that all initiatives, such as audit, resource management and measures of clinical effectiveness, are not stand-alone processes that each require time and effort. Rather they are different aspects of the same drive continuously to improve the quality of health care.

The basic principles associated with the development of clinical audit, whether uni- or multiprofessional, are that the activity should be:

- professionally led
- seen as an educational process
- part of routine clinical practice
- associated with improving quality of care
- based on the setting of standards.

Of course audit should be all of the above, but in this form it is not difficult to understand why the uptake of the government's invitation has been disappointing, as it states the theory quite clearly but says little about practice. 'What's in it for me?' is missing from the theory, yet it is generally recognized that human behaviour is dictated by the most likely reward the behaviour in question is likely to earn. In other words the theoretical benefits of involvement are not as stimulating as a demonstration of how good-quality clinical audit can benefit those involved by helping them to achieve their own aspirations of:

- job satisfaction: delivering best-quality care to patients is the aim of all professionals, and frustrations arise from a perceived inability to do this, whether because of ignorance of what best practice is or obstacles to its attainment

- efficiency: identification of most effective practice usually results in a more efficient process, with the consequent saving of precious time and resources

- effectiveness: the continual search to identify best practice gives health professionals the opportunity to be recognized as the leader in the field.

The Standing Committee on Postgraduate Medical Education (SCOPME)[8] also proposed four key elements and that audit should:

- be directed at quality of care

- include the setting of standards

- compare performances with these standards

- lead to beneficial change.

The first of these elements represents the purpose of audit; the last three represent the three essential steps of the audit cycle, namely set the standard, observe practice, compare it with the standard and implement change.[9]

Russell and Wilson[10] propose a cycle of nine distinct steps for conducting scientific clinical audit, with the caution that effectiveness depends not only on how standards are developed, but also on how they are disseminated and implemented.

1   Choose a general topic for audit and a specific hypothesis to be tested.

2   Develop a standard of care.

3   Disseminate the standard.

4   Implement the standard.

5   Design unbiased and precise methods for sampling patients.

6   Collect valid and reliable data on performance.

7   Compare performance data with the standard by careful statistical analysis.

8   Feed a clear summary of this comparison back to the participants.

9   Ensure that this process generates beneficial change.

All nine steps are of equal importance for good quality audit that everyone involved can sign up to; however steps 2 and 9 have a much greater level of difficulty attached to them, as anyone who has tried to get clinicians to agree to a standard or change their behaviour will testify. Ensuring success in managing change requires a range of interventions, and some judgement will have to be made about which changes require, and are worth, the enormous amount of effort involved. Simply disseminating information will not have the desired effect.[11]

In describing the quality of a service, it must always be compared with something else, either a similar activity or the same activity measured at another time. It also implies measurable consistency over time. Thus quality, as a relative concept, can always be improved, and the process of continual quality improvement is at the heart of all quality initiatives.

All clinical professionals wish to improve the health of their patients through cost-effective and efficient use of resources, and no doubt the vast majority genuinely believe they do. However, as detailed above, less than 20% of medical (let alone clinical) interventions have been formally evaluated in terms of patient outcome and cost-effectiveness. Add to this the fact that our information systems have, until recently, not been sophisticated enough to collect routine data about patients once they have been discharged from acute or community units, and it is hardly surprising that most health care professionals find it hard to accept clinical guidelines from above and prefer to use their 'clinical judgements' on a one-to-one basis with little attention to resource use and opportunity cost.

At the same time we are constantly (and rightly) encouraged to shift the focus of the NHS from the professional to the patient. Ask any patient and an outcome is perceived as 'What happens to me?'. Most patients are aware that data are collected but are not sure which data and therefore assume all. Above all, however, patients assume that clinicians (especially doctors) are all-seeing and all-knowing, and patients would not entertain the thought not only that the effectiveness of their treatment had not been scientifically proven but also that information on outcomes is seldom available unless actively sought, which can be a very resource-intensive activity. Patients also assume that communication between health professionals (especially doctors) is absolute, complete and instant.

The doctor, then, traditionally thinks of quality of treatment and clinical outcomes as that which they can measure (e.g. length of stay, readmission, death or complication rate in the case of the hospital doctor, or for the GP, whether patients come back). Patients (and probably nurses) think of quality of the process of care, and outcomes are that which they experience in terms of symptoms or their relief, disability, physical functioning, anxieties, etc.

There is no doubt that quality is at present a central issue in health care. The challenges, repeatedly emphasized, are there to be seized. In the interests of continually improving the quality of the service, it is essential that doctors and other professional groups, including managers, pick up the challenge and take part in leading the process of change and improvement rather than waiting for change to be dictated from the centre. This approach has been tried and tested.

> Go to the people
> Live amongst them
> Start with what they have
> Build on what they know
> And when the deed is done
> And the mission accomplished
> Of the best leaders
> The people will say
> 'We have done it ourselves'

Lao Tzu

References

1 Secretary of State for Health (1991) *The Patient's Charter* (part of The Citizen's Charter). HMSO, London.
2 World Health Organization (1993) *WHO in a new Europe*. WHO Regional Publications European Series No. 50. WHO, Geneva.
3 Caper P (1988) Defining Quality in Medical Care. *Health Affairs*. 7: 49–61.
4 Smith R (1991) Where is the Wisdom...? *BMJ*. 303: 798–9.

5 McDowell I and Newell C (1987) *Measuring Health. A Guide to Rating Scales and Questionnaires*. OUP, New York.
6 Wilken D (1992) *Measures of Need and Outcome for Primary Healthcare*. Oxford Medical Publications, OUP, Oxford.
7 Bowling A (1991) *Measuring Health*. Open University Press, Milton Keynes.
8 Standing Committee on Postgraduate Medical Education (1989) *Medical Audit – the Educational Implications*. SCOPME, London.
9 Royal College of Physicians (1989) *Medical Audit – a First Report*. RCP, London.
10 Russell I T and Wilson B J (1995) Audit: The Third Clinical Science? *Quality in Healthcare*. 1: 51–5.
11 Jones R, Lydeard S E and Dunleavey J (1993) Problems with Implementing Guidelines: A Randomized Controlled Trial of Consensus Management of Dyspepsia. *Quality in Healthcare*. 2: 217–21.

9 Towards evidence-based practice: the role of research and development, training and education

Stephen Holgate

Research and development in the NHS

In 1988 the House of Lords Select Committee on Science and Technology reported on priorities in medical research[1] and concluded that the NHS needed to be brought into the mainstream of research. The response was the establishment of an NHS research and development (R&D) strategy, led by Professor Sir Michael Peckham.

The achievements of the NHS R&D programme so far include the establishment of eight regional offices of R&D, whose job it is to operate as a 'single centre' to implement the R&D agenda and be sensitive to local needs. Activities include response-mode and commissioned research, training and education, workshops and seminars and dissemination of the findings of research. National advisory groups have reported on NHS R&D priorities in seven areas, with commissioned research already in place in six. The Health Technology Assessment programme, steered by a standing group, has six advisory panels looking at and commissioning research in priority areas.

The UK Cochrane Centre in Oxford is well established and is now part of nine centres in seven countries charged with the remit to facilitate and co-ordinate systemic reviews in the specialized area of randomized control trials.

The NHS Centre for Reviews and Dissemination in York has been established to carry out and commission reviews and updates of research findings on the effectiveness and cost-effectiveness of health care, to maintain and update an international register, to prepare good practice guidelines and to disseminate research-based information effectively.

At each of the regional offices, the NHS R&D Project Register System is soon to be operative to provide easy access to information about work being, or about to be, funded to support management, to provide decision support for new research, to provide a basis for accounting and to capture research overviews.

Following peer review there are now 12 NHS-funded national research units dealing with such topics as social services research, clinical operational research, childhood cancer, perinatal epidemiology, health economics and social policy. A new centre for research and development in primary care has been opened in Manchester. New initiatives for research training awards for nurses and therapists, in the form of studentships and fellowships, have been launched. The DoH itself, through its Centrally Commissioned Research Programme, invested £23.4 × 10^6 in 1993/94.

Supporting R&D in the NHS

As the NHS R&D programme began to pick up speed, it became increasingly apparent that provider units were being asked to provide extra funds to support the excess service costs for undertaking research, especially clinical trials. This in turn created difficulties in implementing trials, even though they might have been of high national priority and have been through rigorous peer review. To deal with this increasing problem, a task force was established in 1994 under the Chairmanship of Professor Culyer from the University of York to investigate a new model for supporting R&D in the NHS. Following the recommendations of the task force report, the government response has been:

- to establish a new 'single' stream funding mechanism for NHS R&D

- the intention to raise R&D funds by a levy on purchasers

- an extra £8 × 10^6 available 1995/96

- a new role for the Central Research and Development Committee (CRDC), advising on how to invest R&D funds

- creation of a National Forum to bring together the major health-related research funders.

R&D: the way forward

In May 1995 a further report by the House of Lords Select Committee on Science and Technology, entitled *Medical Research and the NHS Reforms*,[2] was published. In this a careful review of the progress achieved by the NHS R&D programme was made, as were some recommendations for future development. The overall tone of the report was very positive, accepting that considerable progress had been made. In maintaining the momentum of the R&D programme, several recommendations were made:

- that the regional directors of R&D should continue to play a key role in implementing the R&D strategy but receive help from associate R&D directors. The regional directors should be able to take independent action within their region and foster local research talent

- that response-mode funding would continue and that biomedical projects would not be arbitrarily excluded

- that the regional directors of R&D would retain networking as a top priority, especially in relation to primary care, non-medical scientists and professionals allied to medicine (PAMs)

- that more emphasis be placed on dissemination of R&D findings in appropriate formats

- that, in relation to the Culyer report,[3] due emphasis is given to 'facilities' funding, i.e. the funding of infrastructure activities in research-based institutions that extend beyond project by project support. Any selectivity exercise should be linked to the Higher Education Funding Council exercise currently in place for Universities

- that attempts must be made to preserve 'preprotocol research', and that allowance for curiosity-driven research be built into all NHS R&D activities

- that primary care should receive support from a designated stream

- that the CRDC will be sensitive to science-led approaches to R&D of importance to the NHS

- that the Medical Research Council (MRC) should continue to have first call on NHS resources for service support, subject to a further negotiated 'Concordat'

- that academic centres be permitted to use 'facilities funds' to preserve patient flows necessary for R&D (and teaching), and that purchasers and others concerned in service provision be made aware of the importance of this

- that, as a result of accumulating disincentives to clinical academic careers, an immediate enquiry should be established to investigate how this career track might be improved and supported.

Training and education in the NHS

The 'new NHS' has major elements that will greatly affect the provision of training and education for trainees and consultants. One of these is the purchaser–provider split. Another is the emphasis on moving more health care delivery from the secondary (hospital-based) to the primary care sector, facilitated by joint purchasing agencies or commissions. There are three other changes that will affect the provision of education and research opportunities to the training grades:

- the report of the Chief Medical Officer's Working Group on Specialist Training,[4] which recommends shortening the time a doctor spends in the training grade and an increase in the 'training' content at the expense of 'service'

- the introduction of the NHS Research Development Initiative in 1991 under the direction of Professor Michael Peckham and since January 1996, Professor John Swales, with the prime objective of basing decisions, clinical, managerial and policy, on reliable, research-based information

- the recent publication of the Culyer report *Supporting Research and Development in the NHS*,[3] which recommends greater transparency and accountability of R&D being conducted within the NHS and the identification of a single funding stream that captures both the direct, indirect and excess costs required to conduct research.

Although these changes can in some respects be seen as descriptive, they more importantly provide a unique opportunity to harness training and education, research and development and improved clinical standards into a single integrated exercise.

Implementing best practice

Good clinical practice is absolutely dependent upon practitioners being aware of new developments and how to implement and evaluate them. The powers given to the postgraduate deans working closely with the Royal Colleges will provide new and excellent opportunities for postgraduate and continuing medical education (PME and CME). During the recent review of functions of the new regional offices of the NHS Executive,[5] a clear decision was made not to include the postgraduate deans in the management structure, thereby enabling them to interface more effectively with the higher education institutes, provider units and purchasing authorities.

The potential conflict between the new management structure and training

In setting standards and implementing guidelines of best practice, the post-graduate deans, through their networks, have a major role. However, the regions are being forced to reduce their staff to small numbers (the whole regional office is restricted to 135 staff), which could greatly restrict the capacity of postgraduate deans to function effectively.[5] Having a second 'master' (the purchasers of health care) creates further potential problems; for example the provision of facilities for training and education competing directly with the increased pressure to establish more health care delivery in the primary sector, such as through outreach clinics. Purchasers acting on behalf of their local community may not see PME as a particularly high priority, especially in districts not containing a traditional teaching environment. However it is essential that purchasing authorities see the training of young doctors as a key responsibility upon which the future of the health service depends. A mechanism for maintaining a high profile of this activity in the face of competing (short-term and reactive) demands made upon purchasers is essential if the new powers of the postgraduate deans are to have effect.

Continuing and postgraduate medical education

It is in the interest of all concerned in the delivery of cost-effective and quality health care that PME and CME should be driving the implementation of good practice. Since this forms a central plank of health commissions' functions, a strong local input should be established between the College representatives in the region, the postgraduate dean and the purchasers. This should ideally be closely connected to the provision of clinical advice. In the 'old system', clinical advice came through regional medical advisory committees, with inputs from specialist advisory committees. These structures have now been disbanded or are in the process of being disaggregated in favour of health care advisory groups with strong purchasing input and, in some regions, a health rather than clinical emphasis.

Training and R&D

An emphasis on the rapid throughput of patients, concentration by Trusts on a small number of activities carried out more efficiently, and preferential treatment directed to patients referred from fundholding general practices are all factors that will mitigate against the provision of opportunities for training and education. There is every reason to preserve the well-tried accreditation process whereby the Royal Medical Colleges inspect and approve the training provided by the general and specialist services in hospitals and outreach clinics.

To a large extent PME and CME are dependent upon new information relating to health technologies, clinical practice and the delivery of care. Research has played a major role in the career development of physicians, particularly over the last decade, and a PhD, MD or MS degree has been regarded as a valuable qualification for a consultant appointment. However little attention has been given to (a) the usefulness of the period of 'training' to the subsequent career of the physician, and (b) the usefulness of the research itself to science or to the health base. The Calman reform[4] of clinical training provides little space for experience in research or development. Maybe this is the time to take stock of this aspect of training with respect to the individual whom it is meant to benefit and the provision of a better health service.

The Joint Committee for Higher Medical Training (JCHMT) repeatedly emphasizes the importance of research in the training of all consultants. The mental discipline of research and the ability to assess published material critically is of the utmost relevance in all aspects of medicine. It is important to retain flexibility over the stage at which clinicians in training are able to undertake research. The Calman review[4] points out that the stage of training at which research is undertaken is relatively unimportant. However for applied rather than biomolecular research, relevance to the final career path of the individual is clearly important. The report indicates that there will be no impediment to trainees spending two or three years in a research programme, but emphasizes that at whatever stage this is undertaken, the balance of clinical training must be completed to obtain certification. The postgraduate deans and regional R&D directors will need to play a key role if research experience as part of higher medical training is not to be squeezed out.

The report of the Working Group on Specialist Medical Training[4] states that:

- as a general principle all doctors should acquire basic skills in research methodology, necessary to apply research findings effectively in day-to-day practice

- training in research methodology should be an important and recognized component of all postgraduate training programmes, and that further consideration be given to establishing how this might be achieved

- during the period of general professional/basic specialist training, opportunities for training in research methodology should be identified

- an ability in interpreting and applying research findings and knowledge of research methodologies should be considered when assessing trainees for the award of Certificate of Completion of Specialist Training (CCST).

Putting research into practice

The influence of science upon clinical practice has become increasingly pervasive as the path of technological change has quickened and new frontiers have been explored. Science and technology have contributed many striking advances, but the area of applied research that forms the crucial link between science and its effective application to practice has, until recently, been largely neglected. As a result there has been little attempt to devise a coherent approach to the scientific assessment of health practice methods, no concerted attempt to encourage the systematic use of the results of research and little understanding of how to arrive at and characterize health service problems as research questions. Clinical practice is highly susceptible to fashion and the influence of the enthusiast, and there are many examples of delays in the transfer of important scientific findings into practice.

There is an assumption that health service demand will outstrip available resources and that the gap between supply and demand will grow. What is an effective means of making sound decisions about the content and delivery of health care to secure the best outcomes from investment in health services? The NHS R&D programme is a unique initiative that sets out to provide the basis for rationalization, defined as 'scientific organization of an industry'. This includes the setting of priorities for R&D, the assessment of health technologies (HTA), the commissioning of R&D at both local and national levels to address problems of importance to practice, and setting the necessary structures in place to make use of research findings, to establish a national research database that is accessible to avoid duplication of effort, and to facilitate collaborative links and the systematic transfer of research information (implementation).

Training in research

Applied health research has attracted much less attention than has its biomedical counterpart. For most young clinicians research experience is a laboratory-based or clinical research project, and there has been little interest in providing an alternative experience in health service research or a training in analytical science. Whilst, for the few clinicians who will be pursuing an academic and biomedical scientific career, research focused on the molecular and cellular levels is appropriate, for the majority who will be spending a large part of their time in clinical practice, this experience does not seem appropriate or indeed necessary. There is likely to be a more focused and tailored way than the current PhD/MD/MS route of giving career physicians a critical appreciation of *relevant* research and research methodology to create the sort of evaluative culture envisaged by the House of Lords Select Committee (1989) when it first reported on the state of health science.[2]

A culture has developed more by chance that encourages the acquisition of a PhD, MD or MS on the way to a consultant appointment. Not infrequently trainees embarking on this exercise do so *purely* for the career prospects. The research content is often irrelevant to their future practice, is poorly (or not) supervised and, despite using considerable resources, offers little of relevance to informing or improving any aspect of clinical practice.

The Royal College of Surgeons of England, under the auspices of Professor Hardcastle, has conducted a feasibility study for a Diploma in Clinical Science. Such a diploma would be valuable, *providing* that it was not considered inferior to the more classical MD/MS route. Topics should include research methodology, along with medical ethics; trainees would need to *do* research rather than just learn about it, and there should be a taught component. If doctors of the future are to be sufficiently well informed to play their part in setting priorities and maintaining standards, such a diploma could be invaluable. It would, however, require high-quality teaching staff in adequate numbers and would need to be adequately supervised by the Royal Colleges and the universities.

There is a genuine fear that the strong push being made on health services-related research will erode activity in more basic and biomolecular research. The NHS provides a unique and invaluable resource for conducting this type of research, whether it is laboratory or clinically based. It is, therefore, essential that discussions involving the future of NHS R&D embraces basic and clinical research, for which the UK has an enviable history. The implementation of the Culyer recommendations[3] must take account of this activity if the UK is to become a leader in better health creation. One way forward is to establish more effective relationships between those who have a stake in the more basic aspects of research, including the private sector, so that talented scientists are properly supported and have a clear career structure outside clinical service delivery. For clinical graduates wishing to engage in a research career, it might be more appropriate to encourage the internationally recognized PhD degree rather than the UK MD/MS degree, which causes confusion overseas. Whether or not there should also be a taught component to the PhD is a subject currently being explored by the MRC and the HEFCE.

Clearly if graduates take the more academic route, the clinical content of training will need to be thought about carefully, both with respect to the Calman report on training[4] and to secure routes for career development. Historically there have been a large number of academic chairs and other senior academic posts in medical schools partly or totally funded by the NHS through the old Regional Health Authorities (RHAs). Quite rightly the RHAs considered that this was a wise long-term investment to improve standards through training and research and to encourage an evaluative culture within a specialty. With the devolvement of purchasing decisions to local health commissions and GP fundholding consortia, it is difficult to see what mechanisms will be put in place to protect these posts and, if they are protected, how much their activities will be dictated by purchase-led prioritization. Curiosity-led research and independence of academics in medicine are essential ingredients for innovation, but both of these activities will be seriously threatened if R&D moves more towards goal orientation and direct commissioning.

Managing the 'new NHS' and the conflict between local and national priorities

In managing the 'new NHS' it is indicated that the focus of delivery of care will be at the local level. There are, however, great difficulties in reconciling this with the need to maintain not only national priorities in health care, but also national standards in the training of staff. In order to deliver effective health care, the NHS needs an appropriately well-trained clinical workforce, including doctors and senior medical scientists, who are up-to-date and knowledgeable about the relevance of the products of R&D, the use of clinical audit, the benefits of continuing professional development and appropriate undergraduate and postgraduate training. Policies to ensure that the NHS has such a workforce need to be recognized by purchasers and providers if the services delivered are to be 'state of the art' and delivered by an appropriate skillmix to maximize cost-effectiveness. Maturing purchasers and providers increasingly recognize the benefits of this approach, which would be inappropriate on a purely local basis.

The educational labyrinth

One of the main challenges of handling the transition to a local focus will be to identify what functions need to be co-ordinated and interfaced together to enable the integration of a number of policy initiatives that will achieve a product that is greater than the 'sum of the parts'. The following functions all interconnect: undergraduate medical education (service increment for teaching (SIFT)), PME (including flexible training, junior doctors hours and Calman[4] implementation), CME and continuing professional development (CPD, in which the postgraduate medical dean, associate dean for general practice and dental dean are involved), Working Paper 10 (WP10)[6] for nursing and the professions allied to medicine (undergraduate, postgraduate and continuing professional development), R&D (also links to support research; the Culyer report[3]), medical and clinical audit (which links to continuing education). There would be major disadvantages in some of these functions being carried out independently of each other by a variety of different organizations, such as new regional offices/universities/purchasers/providers.

Undergraduate education, PME and CPD should be provided as a continuum as individuals progress through their career. Hence there needs to be a close co-ordination between the programmes for the research component of SIFT, PME and CPD for nurses, including the use of clinical audit as an educational tool throughout. Close co-ordination of these programmes applies equally to the medical profession within the hospital and community health settings and in general practice. Increasingly these need to be co-ordinated together, with the shift in health care delivery from hospital to community and primary health care settings.

Non-medical health care workers

The same argument applies to clinicians other than doctors. An important educational initiative was put forward under the title of Working Paper 10 (WP10)[6], which already covers undergraduate and some postgraduate training for nurses and other health care professionals. Better co-ordination between different professionals' programmes will reap benefits. CPD needs to be strengthened and focused for all health care workers. In the context of training and education for medical doctors, there is a need for an increase in flexible training, a further reduction of junior doctors' hours, and a review of the skillmix needed to ensure an appropriate and effective clinical workforce. Similarly the introduction of the Calman report[4] will need close co-ordination through the PME system.

The increasing recognition of clinical 'teams' delivering health care in both primary and secondary care also highlights the need for interfaces between the different agencies that are involved. Doctors, nurses, other health care professionals and managers need to share their training programmes, which will only be achieved by integrating and co-ordinating training and health care policies and their implementation. The aim of training and education for any work-force is to be able to deliver an appropriate and up-to-date service. If this is to be achieved in health care, the implementation of the products of R&D must be built into the programmes for CPD, PME and WP10, hence the necessity for links between them. Similarly, educated professionals will continually strive to improve their practice and will generate R&D initiatives, which will need evaluation. The development of knowledge-based purchasing will include utilizing the products of R&D and its evaluation. Hence close links between R&D and education are necessary for co-ordination and greater efficiency.

Supradistrict co-ordination of R&D, training and education

Teaching and R&D need to be co-ordinated at a multidistrict or regional office level. This would deal with functions that require a constituency for action that is larger than either a single provider or a single purchaser, notably where:

- a single purchaser or provider does not have adequate capacity to address the policy issue, or where there are benefits in combining the experience of several providers and purchasers

- implementation of a policy initiative is required for long-term development and support of NHS, but may not be seen as an immediate priority for either purchaser or provider

- scarce skills are involved, so that it is inappropriate, inefficient or not cost-effective to maintain expertise or to 'reinvent wheels' in each provider or purchaser (economy of scale)

- there are advantages in having a supradistrict focus (and economy of effort) in liaison with the centre (NHSE) and other bodies, for example universities

- a supradistrict approach may help to prevent disruption in areas that are currently functioning well or adequately.

Co-ordinated approaches at supracommission level

It can be seen that organization of these functions above the level of purchaser health commissions is necessary in the immediate future (Figure 9.1). It is essential that these supracommission functions continue to implement and co-ordinate policy initiatives and programmes through the 'local

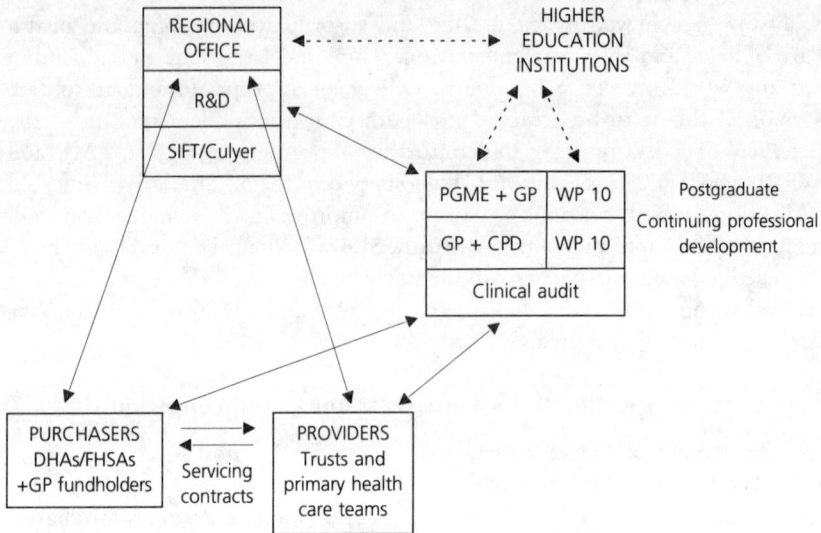

Figure 9.1: Co-ordinated functions at supradistrict level.

expression of the centre' but that they are also grounded in reality, with the programmes aimed to be of benefit to local health service delivery. This can only be achieved by involving the purchasers and providers, including clinicians, in both 'agenda setting' and implementation. The keys to ensuring the delivery of effective health care rest on a well-educated, multidisciplinary clinical work-force, on integrating the products of R&D into change and on an understanding by both clinicians and managers in purchasers and providers as to how these can be achieved.

These functions, programmes and policy initiatives need to be integrated and co-ordinated if we are to achieve the prime responsibility of the NHS, namely to maintain and improve the health of the population through the cost-effective delivery of health care.

The challenge for the next five years is to continue to build upon an already successful and unique programme of R&D in the NHS and to sustain it so that the benefits can be repeated to provide a clear move towards evidenced-based practice in the provision of health care.

Acknowledgement

The author would like to thank Dr Susan Atkinson and Professor John Gabbay for their helpful discussion of the contents of this chapter.

References

1 House of Lords Select Committee on Science and Technology (1988) *Priorities in Medical Research.* HMSO, London.
2 House of Lords Select Committee on Science and Technology (1995) *Medical Research and the NHS Reforms.* 3rd Report. HMSO, London.
3 Culyer A (1994) *Supporting Research and Development in the NHS.* HMSO, London.
4 Calman K (1993) *Hospital Doctors Training for the Future: The Report of the Working Group on Specialist Training.* DoH, London.
5 NHS Executive (1995) *Research and Development in the New NHS: Functions and Responsibilities.* NHS Executive, London.
6 *Working Paper 10.* (1989) HMSO, London.

The context

A fine restaurant owes its reputation not to the freshness of its tablecloths nor to the uniforms of the waiting staff but to the quality and presentation of the food. It is true to say that a number of factors contribute to the overall experience, but if the food is bad, guests will be unlikely to return no matter how friendly the staff or how tastefully appointed the room.

An airline pilot is judged to be good or bad on the basis of whether or not he or she gets the passengers to where they want to be in safety. The amount of leg room or the number of miniature toothbrushes and sleep masks are additional features that may affect the travellers' enjoyment of the flight, but if the airline's safety record is not good, or if the pilots have a habit of flying to the wrong destination, there is a significant risk that passengers will not choose to fly with this company.

The restaurant's greatest resource is the skills and experience of the chef; the airline's greatest resource is the skill of its pilots. In both cases much can be done in terms of technology and procedure to support the final product, but at heart there is the requirement for excellence in the people in charge.

Extrapolating this to the health service, the NHS's greatest resource lies in the skill and expertise of its clinicians. The furnishings of the surgery, the efficiency of the appointments system and the length of the waiting time all contribute to the overall experience. Indeed they cause much irritation to both staff and patients alike when functioning badly. However the essential part of the health service to get right, from both a professional and a managerial perspective, is the knowledge and expertise of the clinicians.

The restaurant with a poor chef will lose customers, and the food in restaurants can be monitored relatively easily. An airline with poor pilots suffers rather more dramatic outcomes. In the health service, the biggest employer in the UK and indeed one of the biggest in Europe, the tracking of poor performance, of outcomes and of adverse events is not yet developed to a sophisticated, uniform level. The situation is further complicated by the multiple factors contributing to any one patient's outcome, by professional tribalism and by tradition.

In common with other professions, for example university teaching or law, standards of clinical practice in the NHS are a matter for external professional bodies and are simply not the domain of managers. Managers have a difficult and complex challenge; they have a responsibility to deliver an excellent service but have no real control over the clinical process. An interesting situation has thus evolved, in which those who hold the managerial responsibility for educating and training the entire work-force, upon which the quality of the clinical service depends, do not generally involve themselves with education of doctors, without whom the service does not function. The profession keeps education very much in its court and has, until recently, been of the view that education at the postgraduate level should be self-directed and entirely a matter for individual choice. As a result some doctors rigorously attend conferences and courses and learn new techniques, whilst others do not.

In June 1994 the Chief Medical Officer, Sir Kenneth Calman, announced his plans[1] for the introduction of continuing medical education (CME), which simply stated that all doctors must undergo a programme of education to keep them up-to-date and abreast of new developments in their specific fields. The Royal Colleges have devised individual plans and schemes tailored to their specialties. The basis of these schemes is to stipulate a minimum amount of education that should be undertaken over a given period. Mechanisms have been developed for monitoring this. The Colleges are working on differing timescales, and the schemes are being introduced as they are being developed.

It is not the fact of CME that causes discussion and debate: the need for clinical staff to be properly educated is unarguable. What has provoked lengthy debate and heated argument is the conflict between the professional and managerial cultures of the NHS, which has been highlighted by the introduction of CME. The aim of this chapter is to provide the reader with some clarity around these issues.

Achieving education whilst still providing a service

Our restaurant owner will train and educate his or her staff during the day time, when the establishment is not open for business. The airline, whose operation must, like the NHS, run 24 hours a day, solves the problem by investing sufficiently in numbers of pilots to allow for a certain proportion to be out of service being educated at any one time.

What then of the NHS? The basic problem is one of providing the service, running the clinics, doing the operating lists, whilst at the same time learning new techniques, reading the literature and generally keeping up-to-date. Traditionally this has been managed very much on an *ad hoc* basis. The clinician decides that a certain conference or course would be interesting or useful. He or she applies for study leave from the clinical tutor or medical director and then sets about finding someone to cover the clinical duties.

The introduction of CME, however, will strain this system in several ways. First, the *ad hoc* arrangements worked as long as a significant number of doctors took less than their allocated number of study leave days. The new system specifies minimum levels of attendance at educational events that are considerably greater than those generally taken. Second, the introduction of the Calman report[2] effectively and quite rightly removes a substantial section of the junior doctor community from service provision, which, in combination with the new deal on junior doctors' hours, puts a further strain on the system.

Each of these initiatives is unarguably sensible as a stand-alone strategy. Problems arise, however, when the combined effects on the clinical service are realized. Significant numbers of clinicians will be needed to keep the clinical service machinery going, and a considerable degree of ingenuity and creativity will be required to attract doctors into the system to fill the gaps.

Medical education or professional development?

There have been two schools of thought on continuing education for clinicians. CME is described by most of the Royal Colleges and refers to a centrally driven scheme that allows doctors to accumulate credit points through attendance at approved courses. Each College sets a minimum number of attendance hours that each doctor must achieve.

SCOPME and the Royal College of Psychiatrists both advocate the adoption of continuous professional development (CPD). The general philosophy is that learning should be a continuous process from entering medical school through to retirement. There should be a gradual transition from learning that is shaped by the needs of the undergraduate curriculum to learning driven by the needs of qualified professionals in a career service post. CPD considers the overall development of each individual. CME constitutes a major part of the process, but CPD also provides strategies for personal coping, professional growth, career development and management skills.

Rather than as two competing entities, CME should be seen as a stepping stone towards CPD. Establishing standards and monitoring systems for the clinical side of the educative process is an essential component that should be seen very much as a part of a long-term commitment to ongoing education and development. The interested reader should review SCOPME's document, *Continuing Professional Development for Doctors and Dentists*[3] for a further discussion of this important issue.

Balancing needs

Individual clinicians have aims and ambitions that they will seek to achieve by means of education. However there is no reason to suppose that these ambitions will coincide with those of their employing organization. An individual may wish to pursue his or her specific interests in an area that does not correspond to the Trust's long-term plans. On the other hand the Trust may decide that a certain service is needed and will be keen to train its staff to be able to deliver the service effectively.

There may also be factors highlighted by the clinical audit process. It may be clear that some areas of the service are weak or indeed that some individuals do not perform as well as others in particular areas. Educative processes may be required to remedy these weaknesses and build up strength and confidence. There may also be national or local educational issues that will warrant investment of time and energy. The clinical tutor, as guardian of the educational resource, will have a view and links with the Royal College advisors and the postgraduate deans, all of whom may have an imperative to implement particular educational processes.

The end result is a difficult and complex balancing act (Figure 10.1). Processes need to be developed to assist doctors and those charged with the task of monitoring CME to devise solutions that best meet these complex demands and needs.

Roles, responsibilities and relationships

The ideal situation is one in which individual clinicians pursue continuous educational activity that is both appropriate to the needs of the service and at the same time does not overly strain the provision of the service itself. In order to achieve this mechanisms must be set up that enable the individual doctor, the Trust and the educational advisors to arrive at a programme for

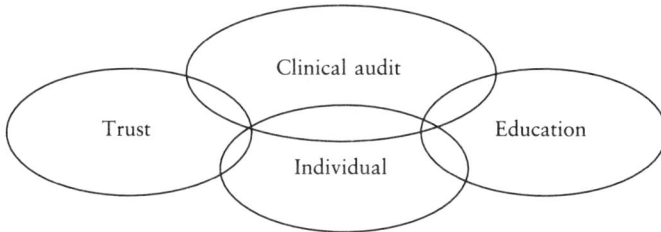

Figure 10.1: Balancing needs. The objectives of the individual in terms of CME must be considered in the light of Trust objectives, performance information brought to light by clinical audit and educational objectives.

CME activity. The decisions cannot be made in isolation by the individual clinician, nor should they be driven solely by the need to hit prescribed CME targets. One way to achieve this would be to create a discussion between the individual, the clinical director and medical director of the Trust, the clinical tutor and the appropriate regional or College advisor. The clinical tutor would provide an educational perspective, the medical director would offer the Trust's needs and strategic direction, whilst the clinical director will have information from the audit process, understanding both the local needs of the directorate and the long-term career aspirations of the individual. Many clinical directors are involved in developing job plans and personal development plans for clinicians, and there is no reason why CME activity should not form a major part of these personal development plans.

The Royal Colleges set standards and define guidelines for the minimum amount of time required to achieve the standards. They also accredit courses provided by other bodies. Postgraduate deans play a major part by taking on roles as negotiators and purchasers of education programmes on behalf of the doctors in their 'patch'.

Putting these interests and influences together results in the model shown in Figure 10.2.

So far the debate on CME and CPD has been largely restricted to the profession itself. However as described in the early parts of this chapter, the education of the clinical work-force is a vital managerial issue, and chief executives and human resource directors will increasingly take an active interest in what has traditionally been a purely professional matter. In most trusts the chief executive, whilst delegating responsibility for CME to the medical director or clinical tutor, will want to see processes in place to make sure that clinical staff all have access to high-calibre medical education.

On the commissioning side, whilst there has been little evidence so far of

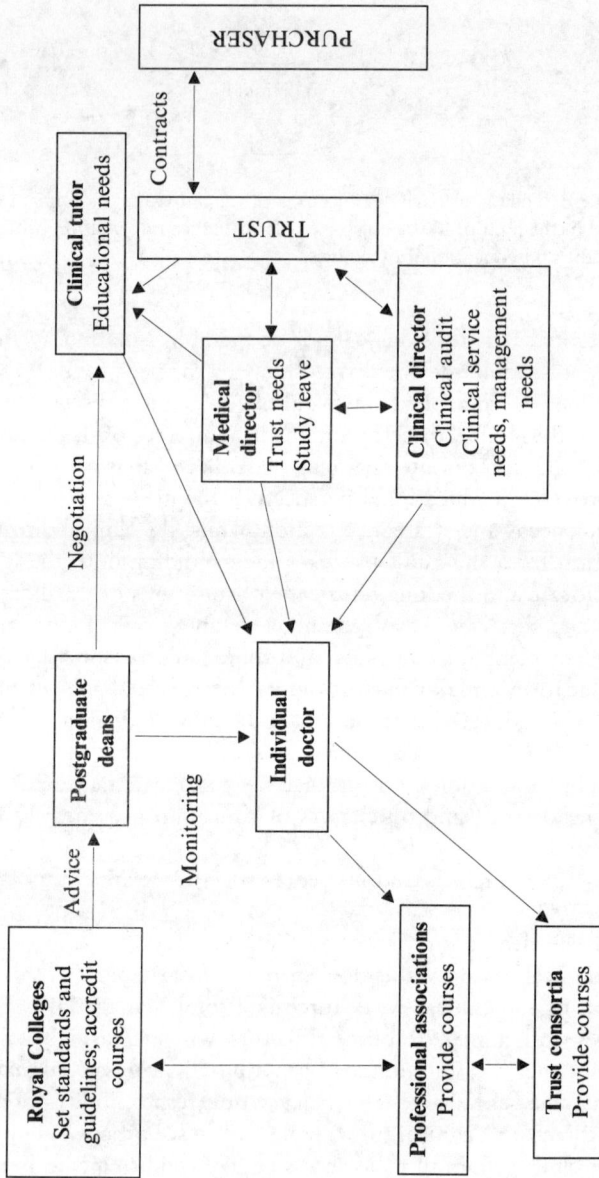

Figure 10.2: CME – the complex model of multiple influences and interests.

interest in CME, it is not at all unforseeable that in the future purchasers will wish to place contracts only with trusts whose consultant staff have been accredited for continuing medical education and development. Indeed this stance and the commitment to back it up by provision in contracts for funding of the CME process could represent an approach to solving the conflict between lack of resource and need to provide training whilst maintaining a service.

Management education for doctors

It would be remiss in a chapter on continuing medical education and development not to include some mention of management education. Traditionally enlightenment on the managerial aspects of the doctor's job has taken the form of a brisk few days at senior registrar level, generally prior to a consultant interview. However there is now a significant body of opinion supporting the view that management education should begin early in every doctor's career, beginning at the graduate level with an understanding of how the NHS works, moving towards a more skill-based approach as the doctor graduates, developing communication and people management skills.

As the doctor's career progresses management education can then expand to some of the more operational and strategic issues; finance, quality management, business planning, negotiation, strategic decision making. It is essential that this learning is backed up by practical experience in all sectors of the health service and at every level, responsibility and work-based projects.

So what do you need to know about CME?

- The process of CME and professional development is essential to the maintenance of high standards and expert practitioners in the NHS.

- The problems are identical to those in any other service industry; that of maintaining a 24-hour service of consistently excellent quality, whilst at the same time educating staff.

- A number of dilemmas are currently the subject of great debate. They are:
  - how to ensure that the service does not suffer
  - CME or CPD – or both?
  - how to ensure that the educational needs of the individual and the Trust are met simultaneously.

- The development of the CME or CPD programme should not be a matter simply for the individual doctor alone; the programme must be developed in light of discussions with the various interested parties.

References

1   Department of Health (1994) *Continuing Medical Education – Consultation Paper*. HMSO, London.
2   Department of Health (1993) *Hospital Doctors: Training for the Future*. Report of the Working Group on Specialist Medical Training (Calman Report). HMSO, London.
3   SCOPME (1994) *Continuing Professional Development for Doctors and Dentists*. SCOPME Working Paper. SCOPME, London.

11   Management arrangements in NHS Trusts

Peter Beck

In 1986 a pilot initiative for management within the NHS was introduced. One of the cornerstones of this resource management initiative (RMI) was to involve 'doctors in management'. This has been welcomed widely throughout the UK, and most units now have a structure that does, to a greater or lesser extent, involve doctors as managers.

The introduction of the NHS reforms, with the 'purchaser–provider' split, has emphasized even more the importance that medical staff have in shaping the development of the NHS; thus the concept of 'doctors in management' has been strengthened even more.

With this emphasis upon management, a new structure has evolved, some of which is statutory, for example the appointment of a medical director and director of nursing to the Trust board, and some of which is discretionary. The latter in particular leads to a variety of models and a variety of job titles across the country, which can be confusing to the uninitiated, especially as many of the different job titles apply to essentially the same job. Most Trusts (provider units) have arrangements that fit into a three-tier management structure (Figure 11.1, Box 11.1), although details will vary between different Trusts.

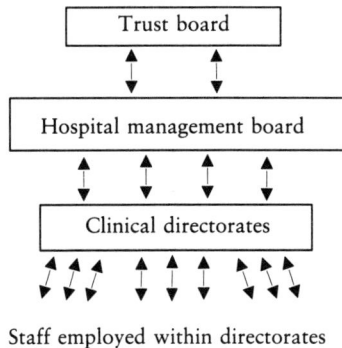

Figure 11.1: The management structure of a trust.

Box 11.1: The three-tier management structure

Trust board: strategic and financial responsibility

Composition	Lay	Chair
		Non-executive directors
	Professional	Chief executive
		Director of finance
		Director of nursing
		Medical director
Functions	Statutory responsibility	
	Setting strategic direction	
	Major policy	
	Ensuring legal/financial control	

Hospital management board: link between strategy and operational management

Composition	Chair: chief executive/medical director
	Executive directors
	Clinical directors
Functions	Development and implementation of policies
	Agreeing and assigning resources
	Business planning

Clinical directorates: responsible for operational management of a clinical area

Composition	Clinical director
	Business manager
	Nurse manager
	Accountant/financial advisor
Functions	Managing and delivering a clinical service
	Managing a budget
	Delivering activity targets related to contracts
	Personnel management
	Health and safety

Communications

In any structure with elements have differing responsibilities, communication becomes vital. Overlapping of membership between the different levels will provide the basis of good communication. Each tier needs to be clear as to its own responsibilities and opportunities within the corporate structure of the Trust.

Roles

The roles of the clinical director and medical director are complementary but with distinct differences (Boxes 11.2 and 11.3).

Box 11.2: The clinical director

Clinical directors are responsible for:

- management of the appropriate clinical area
- all staff within the directorate (excluding 'direct' management of consultants)
- the budget of the directorate
- the quality and effectiveness of the service
- business planning
- marketing and strategic development

Box 11.3: The medical director

The medical director is responsible for:

- providing medical advice to the Trust board/chief executive
- medical strategic development of the Trust
- ensuring the introduction of effective new therapies
- the education and training of medical staff
- policies and procedures relating to medical staff employment, including health and safety, remuneration and discipline
- liaising with purchasers over provision of appropriate medical services

Other groups

There are many other staff groups within the hospital environment that are, directly or indirectly, essential for patient care (Box 11.4).

Some of these groups, for example secretaries and ward clerks, are devolved to and therefore managed by directorates. Some are managed centrally but work in specified directorates; this often applies to dietitians,

---

Box 11.4: Other staff groups

Clinical support staff

- Physiotherapists
- Occupational therapists
- Dietitians

Hotel staff

- Catering
- Domestic
- Porters
- Laundry

Clerical and administrative

- Secretaries
- Ward clerks
- Medical records
- Personnel

Estates

- Designers
- Engineers
- Maintenance

---

occupational therapists and physiotherapists. Some are managed externally to the Trust, having been subjected to 'market testing'; this applies especially to domestic, portering and laundry services.

Other responsibilities

Over and above the provision of health care are a number of other vital functions that have a major impact upon the clinical environment. Of particular importance to medical staff are the following.

Postgraduate medical education (PME)

The responsibility for this lies with the clinical tutor (director of postgraduate medical education (DPGME)). The DPGME (Box 11.5) is accountable to the postgraduate dean, employed through the university. The latter 'holds' the budget for PME for trainees. This accounts for 50% of the total salary of juniors in training, the other 50% being held by Trusts for the service element of juniors' work. In Scotland 100% of a junior's salary is held by the postgraduate dean. In removing all of the salary budget for trainees, the postgraduate deans have considerable power to ensure that trainees receive proper structured training and are not abused. The introduction of maximum rotas and detailed training specification, including weekly study time, have, however, impacted greatly upon service delivery to the extent that some units have become non-viable and either cannot train junior staff

---

Box 11.5: Director of postgraduate medical education

The director of postgraduate medical education:

- holds the budget for junior medical trainees (training element)

- ensures an adequate training programme

- approves appropriate study leave

- provides counselling/assessments

- audits PGME

- has involvement in continuing medical education for career grade staff

---

or have had to join with neighbouring units to achieve the critical mass to survive.

Compulsory continuing medical education (CME) has been introduced into the consultant contract, placing another constraint upon medical staff time and therefore upon service delivery (Chapter 10).

Clinical audit

This is an obligation for all clinicians and is increasingly being enforced by purchasers through the contracting process. The aim is clearly to improve the quality and effectiveness of clinical care, and the responsibility rests with a variety of staff including:

- the medical/clinical audit chairman
- the medical director
- the director of quality/nursing.

Risk management

This covers all of the risks that a Trust faces, including buildings, security, damage and personal liability. For the medical staff, complaints, clinical negligence and litigation are central concerns. It may be the responsibility of any one of a variety of staff, often falling to the medical director.

Tensions

For the doctor within a Trust setting, there are numerous tensions associated with the requirements of the present NHS. Especially prominent is the potential conflict between the needs of the individual patient and the needs of the population at large. For the doctor in management, there are pressures to maintain the service as a whole versus his or her commitment to patients. In addition there are the time pressures involved in performing what appear to be two distinct and equally exacting roles.

Summary

The structure of the new NHS as described in this 'skeleton' has brought together a number of different health service professionals in a way never before achieved. This provides the opportunity for 'tribal barriers' to be broken down and for the professions to work together to improve the quality of patient care. Doctors have to understand and be involved in those changes in order to ensure that their role in the changed NHS is achieved to the full.

Glossary

Structure

Trust board

The legally responsible entity for running an NHS Trust. Responsible for ensuring that financial and other targets are met. Responsible for overall strategic direction of the Trust and ensuring its long-term viability. Composed of a chairman, executive directors and non-executive (lay) directors.

Hospital management board

Responsible for ensuring that business plans of the Trust are drawn up and met, resources allocated appropriately, and appropriate policies and procedures developed. Usually comprising clinical directors together with chief executive and other executive directors.

Clinical directorate (clinical management team)

A small group responsible for the day-to-day running and planning of a specific clinical area, specialty or small groups of specialties. Usually led by a consultant (clinical director), supported by a general manager, nurse manager and accountant.

Function

Business plan

Developed annually. Describes the plans that the Trust has in terms of activity, quality, finance and new developments. Forms the basis for the Trust's contract with its purchasers.

Strategy

Usually developed over five years. Gives the direction and aims of the Trust over a longer period, taking into account anticipated medical developments, patient requirements, available funding and other constraints. Forms the basis for the annual business plan.

Personnel

Chairman

Lay member appointed by the Secretary of State to chair the Trust board. Usually has significant connections geographically or functionally with the Trust and brings external business skills to the Trust.

Chief executive

Has overall responsibility for the running, and development, of the Trust. Responsible for implementing major policy decisions and for the employment and monitoring of senior managers.

Clinical director

Usually (but not always) a consultant who is responsible for the day-to-day running and planning for a specific clinical area, specialty or group of specialties. Responsible for employment and monitoring of all staff within his or her clinical management team, including junior medical staff. May or may not be given specific management sessions to undertake the role; usually continues full-time clinical commitment.

Medical director

An executive director of the Trust board. Responsible for giving medical advice to the Trust. Overall responsibility for medical developments within the Trust. Sets policies for medical staff. Works closely with clinical directors. Usually works on a part-time basis as medical director whilst maintaining clinical commitments.

Business manager (general manager, directorate manager, clinical service manager)

Responsible for the day-to-day running of a clinical service on behalf of the clinical director. Often shares a number of clinical management teams. Usually works alongside, or is managerially responsible for, a nurse manager.

Nurse manager

Responsible for the day-to-day management of nursing staff within a clinical management team. Usually also responsible for quality initiatives. May share the role with, or be accountable to, the general manager.

12 The medical director: corporate player, not representative role

Tim Scott

Created by statute

It is interesting to speculate on what was going on in Richmond House during those heady days in 1988 when the White Paper[1] was being written. The Secretary of State, ministers and officials seemed to make almost daily trips to Downing Street, where the critical elements of the reforms were being put in place. Trust hospitals were central to this, but to what extent people thought at all about the management of those organizations and the particular role different individuals within the Trust board might play is lost in history. Certainly the first wave of NHS Trusts received very particular and special attention, not only from the newly formed Trusts Unit within the NHS Management Executive (as it then was) but also from ministers and the Secretary of State. This attention, however, focused almost entirely on the selection of the chairman and chief executive. The balancing non-executive members were seen largely as a compromise between shifting the orientation towards a more business-like approach and the necessity for keeping local community and patient group interests on board. The executive positions were also agreed relatively simply. Although at one point the Healthcare Financial Management Association (HFMA) girded its loins to fight the good fight if treasurers were left off the board, there can have been very little discussion about the need for a director of finance to be a full voting member of the Trust board. Similarly, with both the BMA and RCN in truculent mood, it would have been suicidal to suggest that there would not be a doctor or a nurse on every Trust board. And so the role of medical director was created and statutorily recognized.

Initial appointments

What is interesting, searching back through records of the times, is the almost complete lack of any prescriptive guidance on what the role of that individual might be. It seems very clear that that level of detail had not concerned those who set the NHS on its brave new course.

Of course medical directors were not just appointed on the day a unit became a Trust. Detailed research and interviews[2] indicate a fairly similar pattern in the majority of cases. A unit would start a gradual and tentative movement towards Trust status, viewed, particularly for those in the first wave, as a highly politicized action. There would almost inevitably be some temperature taking amongst medical staff. In fact in a considerable number of hospitals, a formal ballot was taken of the medical staff to determine whether or not they wished to move to Trust status. This was often a highly political game; the ballot was in many ways a vote of confidence or otherwise in the existing general manager, and general managers' careers often rode on the results. 'After all, if he can't deliver the doctors, how's he ever going to be able to run a Trust!' was the cry to be heard in Richmond House. In some hospitals the inner group of doctors, managers, nurses and others who did their best to preserve the hospital from excess of any sort would wisely counsel that the hospital was not a genuine candidate for the first wave and persuade chairmen, both district and regional, to give them a little breathing space. In others things were pushed to the limit, sometimes with unhappy results.

In those likely to achieve first-wave Trust status, the manager leading the process, usually the project manager of the first-wave Trust project, would need to ensure that a doctor would emerge to take on the medical director role. NHS Trust application forms had a box that needed ticking, 'Doctors are involved in management', and the achievement of this required leadership from amongst the medical community.

The way in which this process developed is a fascinating topic in its own right. During the research I talked to a number of medical directors who reluctantly took on the role and for whom the clinching argument was their colleagues' grave concerns about who might otherwise accept the job if they did not. One tactic adopted by some managers and chairmen was to hint at one or two outrageous potential candidates in order to accelerate the acceptance of the need for a medical director. Of course the people whose names were considered were those who already had considerable managerial and political experience. Those who had served on district management teams (DMTs), as consultants on DHAs, as medical executive committee (MEC) chairmen and so on were the likely candidates. The usual political compromises would take place between the major clinical power groups in trying to ensure that a 'balanced' candidate took on the role.

Even at this stage doctors and others began to realize that this was not the kind of post that doctors had taken before. Most chief executives made it clear that whilst they respected the rights of the medical community to identify suitable candidates, they would be appointed, or not, by the chief executive, the chairman and the Trust board. In some hospitals the chief executive had made it quite plain on an informal network that certain individuals would be unacceptable and, even if nominated, would not be appointed. In one or two hospitals this actually happened; the doctors nominated an individual who was rejected by management, with the result that the doctors had to go through the process for a second time. Shadow Trust boards were at this state fairly nebulous, with a chairman and chief executive usually being the powerful duo who were bringing together a balance of forces to shape and drive the Trust. They were, of course, in constant dialogue with Richmond House, and the power and influence of districts and regions was very considerably reduced from that which they had enjoyed in the past. For many of the hospitals and units involved, this was a very novel experience, and there is no doubt that the first generation of medical directors, and indeed the other executive members of the Trust boards, felt that they were, in some sense, trailblazers.

Early challenges

What early challenges did these new medical directors take on? For many the simple role during the run up to Trust status was to hold the clinical body together, i.e. to continue to ensure that the majority of medical staff were kept abreast of developments and continued to support the move to Trust status. For others, where the situation was perhaps a little less volatile, the most urgent task was working with the chief executive, either to devise and implement or to consolidate and develop some form of clinical directorate structure, in which doctors would play a visible and acknowledged role in the management of the organization. This again was part of ticking the DoH's boxes, and may in some units have resulted in little more than well-painted scenery.

For many, to their surprise, one of the most pressing tasks was to try to agree some form of contract, negotiate and agree some form of reward, organize some sort of support and generally create a post from scratch. Even now, as research evidence makes abundantly clear, there are enormous variations in all aspects of the medical director's role, even within relatively similar Trusts. It will be the twenty-first century before there is any degree of comparability and reasonable uniformity between Trusts, allowing for the unique and different roles medical directors are playing. Peter Brown, Medical Director of Milton Keynes, has talked eloquently about how one of his central objectives over his period as medical director has been to formalize and structure the post in such a way that it can not only attract a successor but also give that person some kind of framework and support.

Lastly, of course, medical directors, in common with all other Trust executives, found themselves going through the inevitable developmental dynamics of the establishment of a new team. Most Trust boards contained a variety of individuals who were new to each other and often had disparate ambitions and objectives, and it is easy to identify the classic stages of 'forming, storming, norming and performing' as these individuals began to learn how to function as a group.

Corporate responsibility

In the midst of all this, however, what was perhaps most challenging for medical directors as individuals was the understanding of, and assumption of, corporate responsibility.

The Cadbury Report on corporate governance had been issued[3], but even prior to that the Trust Unit at the DoH had been pressing the issue of accountability on Trust boards. A variety of training organizations offered specific programmes for management teams to consider and develop this aspect of their work, and the item was up in the air everywhere. In 1994 I interviewed Brian McGucken, Medical Director of Wigan & Leigh NHS Trust. He described in some depth the difference he had experienced between an intellectual appreciation of what corporate responsibility meant and the genuine internalizing of that concept. He could, in retrospect, see how over a period of perhaps a year he had moved from only participating in Trust board discussions where matters that were either clinical or linked to medical staff were discussed, to the position where he felt able to contribute to any agenda item and acknowledged his responsibility for all decisions. The way he described it the responsibility came first, with the contribution coming second. 'I began to realise that if we made a decision about staff bonus, I was party to that decision, and later became confident that I had something to contribute to the discussions, not because I was a doctor, but because I was a member of the Trust board in my own right as an individual'.

That this process took so long to internalize is perhaps not surprising when we look at the historical role of doctors. In the first place, for at least the past 20 years, the formal role of many medical staff within the NHS was, as Sandy Macara, Chairman of the BMA, observed[4], 'rather like the Greek chorus – commenting on the action, but not participating in it'. The chairman of the MEC would sit on the DMT and formally voice the concern of his or her colleagues over what was going on in the district. Thus there was already a history of representative roles.

Second, any one professional, if the sole member of that profession within a group, feels impelled in some respects to act as a representative of that profession. Thus, even if not formally taking on a representative role, a doctor will feel the need to speak for doctors if he or she is the only doctor present. This of course relates not merely to professional roles but also to any distinctive characteristic, and an isolated and sole woman within a group will often feel pressured to speak for women as a group in a way that she would not were there two or more women present. Thus, social theory suggests that medical directors are pushed into making representative remarks, which may again make it more difficult for them to shift perspective.

Third, there have been, and may still be, occasions on which it was not in the interests of the administrative management staff genuinely to encourage participation of other members of the executive team. It may well have suited their interest to encourage doctors and nurses to continue to see themselves as offering professional advice, and to discourage them in a variety of ways from participating in other operational and strategic decisions. It has been clear from the early days of resource management that if doctors are to increase their participation in management, someone is going to decrease theirs! Regrettably, not all chief executives have been mature enough to make that space, and medical directors have not always understood corporate responsibility. For Simon Baugh, Medical Director of Bradford Community Trust, the moment of truth came when the Trust board began to discuss indemnity insurance for Trust board members. 'I realized that I was going to be sharing and making some potentially major business decisions, and the fact that I would need insurance in case we made a mistake dramatically highlighted to me my individual role in all this'.

If medical directors are not in any sense to be seen as representatives of the medical staff, who, if anyone, can play that role, and does that role need to be taken forward? Some Trusts have a model whereby a medical staff group continues to meet, albeit relatively infrequently, and elects its own chair to speak for medical staff. In these Trusts this has been encouraged by management by including the individual as a participating member of the management team, although not as a statutory and voting member. Not only does this have the obvious effects of clarifying the role of the medical director whilst retaining the voice of the medical staff, it also has the added advantage of ensuring that the medical director is not the sole doctor in the room. This takes a personal weight off the shoulders of the medical director and often enables both doctors to speak more freely.

Reaction of colleagues

A further problem in the shift from representative to corporate board member, has been the expectations of consultant colleagues. Many medical directors have described to me the dismay registered by other colleagues who have attempted to use the medical director in the traditional way as a mouth piece for their concerns. 'Do have a word, and get them to do something about the renal clinic will you John?', is beginning to fall on deaf ears, as consultants find that the medical director is taking a determined and corporate stance with their Trust board colleagues. In this respect it is interesting to look at the pattern of relationships between clinical directors and medical directors in the vast majority of trusts that have a clinical management structure.

Current postholders

Who then do we find taking on the role? Some early gossip suggested it was largely consultants nearing retirement, particularly drawn from such specialties as anaesthetics, pathology and radiology.

The evidence does not support this. Nearly half (47%) are between 41 and 50 years of age, and specialties are represented proportionally, with general medical specialties dominating (29%). Not surprisingly within community Trusts we found that 62% of medical directors were psychiatrists, but otherwise no group dominated. Regrettably there does seem to be gender bias; only 13% of medical directors are female, compared with 17% of the consultant body as a whole.

Only 6% of medical directors had any management qualifications, ranging from Masters degrees to diplomas.

Key relationships and structures

What are the structural relationships between the chief executive, the medical director and the clinical directors in those Trusts with a directorate management structure? Two possible models are set out in Figure 12.1. In the first the medical director is accountable to the chief executive, as are the clinical directors. The BAMM research found this in 56% of all Trusts. In the second model the clinical directors are accountable to the medical director, who is in turn accountable to the chief executive. This was the case in 12% of Trusts. Even within these two basic models, we find all sorts of subtle variations. For example some medical directors state that they are accountable to the Trust board rather than the chief executive, and so on. However from the perspective of the clinical director, these models are very similar.

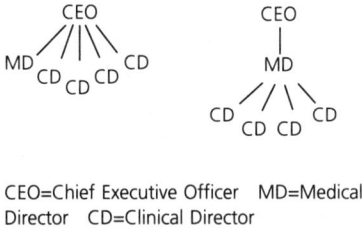

CEO=Chief Executive Officer   MD=Medical Director   CD=Clinical Director

Figure 12.1: (above) Two models of the managerial relationships between the chief executive and the clinician managers.

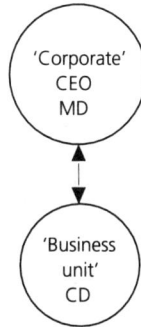

Figure 12.2: (right) Relationship between 'corporate' trust management and clinical directorates.

CEO=Chief Executive Officer   MD=Medical Director   CD=Clinical Director

Whatever organizational charts say about relationships between individuals, what matters is the relationship between 'corporate' and 'business unit' (Figure 12.2). That is in a Trust with a devolved management structure, there are a series of business units, usually called clinical directorates, which actually provide health care and deliver the contracts into which the organization enters, and some form of corporate body, the Trust management committee or similar, which brings together the business units within a single organization, shares risk amongst them, so that those with particular problems can be assisted and supported by those who are currently successful, takes overall responsibility for the balance between the business units and seeks to identify and enhance synergy between business units.

Professor Michael Porter put it succinctly for the business world when he said, 'Corporate doesn't compete in the market place, only the business units do!'[5] In the NHS, Trust boards do not deliver clinical service but may sign the contracts guaranteeing to deliver it; only the clinical directorates can

deliver clinical service. This of course raises a whole series of questions about
the role of corporate in a devolved organization. Porter makes it clear that if
corporate does not provide any 'added value' to the business units, they
might just as well stand free. Chris Bunch, Medical Director of the Oxford
Radcliffe Hospital NHS Trust says, 'Trust Boards, and in particular medical
directors, need to think carefully about what added value they bring to the
patient/clinician encounters going on every day in all their directorates'.

If we think about these two elements, the corporate group and the
directorate group, and the relationship and processes between them, we can
defuse some of the personal issues inherent in normal organizational accountability diagrams. What is important is that there are responsibilities
and accountabilities in both directions between the directorate group and the
Trust corporate group, and within that the medical director and clinical
director play critical roles.

In one Trust the key process was described to me as follows. There is an
annual meeting between the chief executive and the clinical director, with the
medical director 'sitting in'. This meeting is a formalization of the agreement
between the directorate and corporate as to what resources will be made
available to the directorate and the service that they will deliver on receipt of
those resources. This clearly ties to contracts that have been agreed with
purchasers, but there may not be a specific link. Having established the basis
of the agreement for the coming year, which might be termed a business
plan, the corporate group will then routinely monitor some kind of performance figures in order to determine the extent to which the directorate
group is diverging from the expected pattern. The importance of any kind of
plan is to provide a baseline from which to measure variance, which will
inevitably occur. A written plan also serves as a series of tentative notes,
picking up some specific aspects of what is usually a much more complex
shared understanding of what will happen, between corporate and directorate.

At around six months into the year, there would be a further formalized
meeting between the medical director, the clinical director and probably a
number of specific staff from within the directorate. This meeting would
focus on both the current performance against the plan and the implications
for plans for the following year. Again the word 'plans' should be interpreted
to mean not merely, and not only, pieces of paper with numbers written on
them but also a shared understanding of changes in the volume, nature and
style of service being offered.

In setting out this model for me, the medical director involved laughingly
commented that he and the chief executive could play 'the nice policeman
and the nasty policeman' and in fact vary the roles between them. Usually he
was the 'nice policeman', so that the meetings where he alone appeared

allowed the directorate team to be a bit less formal and admit some of the problems they were having, putting him in the position of facilitator and support, whereas those meetings with the 'nasty policeman' present were more about ensuring corporate contributions and allegiance from the directorates group. He also admitted, which I think is important, that with some directorates he and the chief executive took the reverse role. It obviously depended to some extent on personality and also on his own clinical specialty and its relationships to the different directorates. It was essentially arbitrary and a matter of management style, since in the end the meetings boiled down to a meeting between a person or people from the corporate group and a person or people from the directorate, and colleagues had very quickly learned that in the end he and the chief executive carried the same agenda and vision.

The majority of clinical directors are accountable to the chief executive[2] and do not have any responsibilities to the medical director. In fact the majority of medical directors have few if any staff at all accountable directly to them, often just a handful, centred around audit staff. I have asked many medical directors, given these circumstances, how they see their relationships to clinical directors. The descriptions I am given often centre around words like 'coach', 'support', 'a shoulder to cry on', 'an advisor' and so on. As one of them put it to me, 'The clinical directors know what needs to be done in their own directorates and I know what we need to do to run the business'. Whilst some medical directors successfully combine the role with that of clinical director, particularly in relatively small Trusts, others, particularly in large Trusts, have told me that this would be absolutely fatal, compromising their position as medical director and making their position as a working clinician untenable.

Clinical work

This last point is perhaps the most important of all; '76% of all medical directors work five or more clinical sessions'.[2] If any one single fact stands out in the research to date it must be this one. The only member of the Trust board who is consistently likely to be working on a routine daily basis with patients is the medical director, and therein, of course, lies their enormous strength and value and the core dilemma, which they can never resolve but must continue to manage, between the good of the organization and the needs of the individual patient.

References

1 Department of Health (1989) *Working for Patients* (Cmnd 555). HMSO, London.
2 BAMM (1995) *Medical Directors–The Key to the Future?* BAMM Cheadle.
3 Cadbury Committee (1994) *The Report of the Committee on the Financial Aspects of Corporate Governance.* HMSO, London.
4 Macara S (1994) Foreword in *Management of Hospital Doctors* (eds M Burrows, R Dyson and P Jackson *et al.*), *Butterworth Heinemann, Oxford.*
5 Porter M E (1989) How competitive forces shape strategy, in *Readings in Strategy Management* (eds D Asch and C Bowman), Open University Press, Buckingham.

13 The clinical director: poacher turned gamekeeper?

Celia Cramp

The concept of a medical consultant who is also managerially responsible for the running of a unit is nothing new. The medical superintendent role was created before the NHS came into being, only to be replaced by administrative staff as major decision making passed to district and regional health authorities. Consultants had considerable autonomy when organizing their individual work practices, both inside and outside the hospital, but at a hospital level, administrators controlled day-to-day affairs. Many services changed and grew according to the enthusiasms and skills of individuals rather than in response to either public demand or health need.

Why have clinical directorates (and clinical directors)?

The need to change individual consultant attitudes to work practices was probably the primary reason for setting up clinical directorates when hospitals changed to a more market orientation with the advent of the purchaser–provider split (Box 13.1).

Box 13.1: Why have clinical directors?

- To allow consultants to use their clinical knowledge to influence service provision: the *power*

- To pass *responsibility* to consultants for doctors' co-operation with management

- To give authority and respectability to the new management system: the *appearance*

Sceptics would say that the clinical director was needed primarily as a figurehead to make the reforms work, given plenty of responsibility for achieving some difficult changes but very little extra power to make things happen. In reality the reforms have been implemented in many different ways in different units, so the role, power and responsibilities vary considerably from unit to unit. The power is often indirect, the position giving opportunities to influence decisions more often than it gives the ability to make them. Some consultants who have taken on this role have become disillusioned, but I have found that it is possible to achieve changes that improve patient care and allow professional staff to influence the shape of services, as well as provide them. In some Trusts the clinical director goes under a different title, such as lead professional, but the role is usually similar.

The directorate team

A clinical director who attempts to manage a directorate alone will spend far more time on this activity than can usually be released from clinical commitment. It is essential to have a team in which roles are clearly defined (Box 13.2). The members of this will vary from Trust to Trust but will almost always include some nurse management (either at directorate or ward level) and some financial skill (business manager and accountant). Monitoring of activity against contract may be left to the clinical director, but he usually has some help with this. Last, but certainly not least, he will need some secretarial assistance. In some units this is left to the clinical director's medical secretary, but a personal assistant can be much more productive in taking over most of the paperwork and organizational aspects of the department, as well as the secretarial component of the work.

This group will usually meet regularly as a team with other consultants and ward managers to form the directorate management group, sometimes referred to as a directorate management team. This is an important route for communication within the directorate and a means of joint decision making. There is often a junior medical representative on this group, most commonly a senior registrar. This allows the directorate the benefit of a junior medical opinion and also allows the senior registrar to gain some experience in directorate management. The senior registrar should take the opportunity to be an active member of the group as part of his training in the skills required of a consultant. He should share the minutes of this meeting with the other junior doctors and act as a channel for their views. In other units a bulletin of the main decisions of the group will be published widely within the directorate.

Box 13.2: Clinical directorate team

Clinical director	• Figurehead and overall manager of the directorate
	• Acts as medical lead
	• Carries the prime responsibility for communication
Nurse manager	• Manages nursing staff (replaced by ward managers in some hospitals)
Accountant	• Assists with budget management (may be replaced by business manager)
Business manager	• Assists with budget management
	• Monitors activity against contract
	• Looks for business opportunities for the directorate
Contracts manager	• Monitors activity against contract (when there is no business manager)
Departmental tutor	• Organizes junior medical staff training (assessments, tutorials)
	• May organize junior medical staff rotas
	• Organizes medical students within the directorate
Personal assistant to clinical director	• Provides administrative and secretarial support to the clinical director and sometimes to other members of the directorate team

Many of these functions are likely to be part time. Members of the team will therefore have other duties, particularly clinical responsibilities, or be shared between two or more directorates

Responsibilities of the post

The responsibilities divide into two parts, which can on occasions be difficult to reconcile (Box 13.3). The first is to act as champion for the directorate

---

Box 13.3: Clinical director duties

Within the directorate	• Involve staff in planning
	• Manage departmental secretarial services
	• Manage the departmental budget
	• Plan departmental activity and write the annual business plan
	• Monitor departmental activity against contracts and take action if these are not being followed
	• Personnel issues: hiring and firing (limited in practice to non-consultant staff)
	• Keep departmental staff informed about what is going on – within the directorate – within the Trust
	• Organize junior medical staff
Within the Trust	• Act as a corporate member of the clinical management team
	• Represent the directorate
With other agencies	• Be involved in contracting with purchasers
	• Seek out ideas and opinions (GPs, patients, other service users) and incorporate these in planning

The clinical director is largely responsible for the directorate's image, both inside and outside the Trust

---

within the Trust and manage the directorate resources, both staff and budget, to achieve the best possible service. The second is to form part of the corporate management structure of the Trust, a role in which another directorate's priorities must sometimes be supported if it is in the best interests of patient care as a whole. Most clinical directors coming into post for the first time find the latter task harder than the former, especially since, in order to retain the support of consultant colleagues within their directorate, they must be seen as having the best interests of that directorate at heart.

When clinical directors are first appointed, they are usually seen by other members of staff as the holder of the purse-strings. Responsibility for the unit budget is important and is often seen by the chief executive as the marker for success or failure in the post. An astute clinical director will use money to oil the wheels of change rather than regard a balanced budget as his sole priority. When expenditure is clearly about to exceed income, the budget becomes the impetus for change, either by increasing income or decreasing expenditure. Many service innovations have been implemented as a creative response to these dilemmas. Planning ahead for such eventualities is one of the key marks of a successful manager.

Contract income is the basis of the clinical director's budget. The greater his involvement in the contracting process, the fewer the nasty surprises later in the year when work has to be carried out within the budget agreed. A clinical director's contract negotiations begin with his colleagues in his own department when he discusses consultant job plans and the amount of work that can be done, on both an individual and a departmental basis. He must be aware of other relatively fixed resources, such as bed and theatre session availability, and may need to negotiate changes in his department's access to these with other clinical directors. The strength of clinical director involvement in contract negotiations with the purchasers lies in this understanding of what he can reliably provide, together with his clinical knowledge. This enables him to talk about patient care first and money second, with a degree of authority that no accountant can match. For this reason, clinicians are usually regarded as valuable members of contracting teams, although in some Trusts this is left to the medical director rather than individual clinical directors.

A successful clinical director involves his directorate in their own management in three main ways:

- keeping them fully informed of what is going on

- encouraging free and open discussion of ideas, especially if these are controversial

- involving them in major decisions.

The key skills needed are those of communication, management of change and the ability to see the way ahead. These are much harder to acquire than is the technical knowledge needed to write a business plan, present a business case, hire and discipline staff, match resources to activity and read the budget sheet. There are often other staff who have knowledge of specific areas who can help with these practicalities of management. I will illustrate these principles with an example that will probably sound familiar to many clinical directors.

The problem

The waiting time for a first outpatient appointment within a specialty has risen from ten weeks to 19 weeks. This is outside the Patient's Charter standard of 13 weeks, and the Trust risks penalties from its major purchasers. Some GP fundholders have threatened to take their patients elsewhere if the waiting time is not reduced to a maximum of eight weeks.

Action

Look at the reasons for the change in waiting time. The answer to this may dictate appropriate remedies. Possibilities include:

- cancelled clinics due to:
  - a temporary problem (staff on leave or study leave, bank holidays)
  - a long-term problem (long-term sickness, changes in junior doctor availability to assist in clinics)

- fewer patients being seen in clinics due to:
  - changes in booking schedules. If so, have booking schedules been altered to cope with rising revisit ratios, to achieve Patient's Charter standard or because individual consultants feel they are being pushed too hard or wish to shorten their clinic sessions?
  - increase in non-attendance rates. (This has the double effect of reducing the number of patients seen in the clinic where they were originally booked and of using slots in future clinics for rebookings if the appointment is remade.) If so, why? Is a different method being used to notify appointments? Are timings less convenient than they used to be because they (or the times of the buses for example) have changed? Is one particular clinic involved? If so, are patients dissatisfied?

- rising demand. If so, where does it come from? Fundholders or non-fundholders? Do your contracts allow you to obtain extra income for this increased work?

Always ask, 'Is the cause temporary or permanent?'
Remember that more than one cause may co-exist.

- Look at possible action. This can be a short-term remedy if the reason for the increase has now passed, but will need to be more fundamental if the reason persists. Make sure that solving one problem does not create another, such as an unacceptable increase in waiting times between listing and surgery if patients are seen rapidly in the outpatient clinic on referral.
  Short-term possibilities:
  – the consultant concerned to do a few extra clinics
  – another consultant to do a few extra clinics (use waiting list monies?)
  – more junior doctor time in clinic instead of on the wards or in theatre.
  Long-term possibilities:
  – another regular clinic (need to consider all consultants job plans)
  – move clinics off Mondays (bad for bank holidays)
  – reduce the follow-up rate. Consider joint protocols of management with referring GPs.

- Discuss all your findings and possible solutions with those concerned with provision of clinics. They must understand why you need to address this problem and not simply be faced with your solution. The latter approach usually results in unhappy staff and failure to resolve the problem. Consultants should expect help from their clinical director in managing their contribution to solving this crisis, rather than just demands for more activity.

- Organize appropriate and agreed change. This may involve seeking extra resources or redeploying those you have.

Is this for you?

Some senior registrars will go forward into a consultant post with no wish to fill a managerial role; others have more inclination to be involved in this way. I would advise all senior registrars to ask their clinical director to give them some experience of management issues (attend the departmental and hospital management groups, help with some managerial tasks for example) so that they may form their own views. The system of 'Buggins' turn' for clinical director is unsatisfactory for a Trust, a department and Buggins! If you have an interest, develop your knowledge of how things are done and improve your skills in management of time, people and change. When you have settled into a consultant role, you may well find yourself being asked to consider a clinical director post. It does take time away from clinical practice (on average two or three sessions each week), and on many occasions you will be glad to return to direct patient care as patients are so much more grateful for your efforts than your colleagues seem to be. If you take the plunge I wish you success. If you choose instead to concentrate on patient care, research or private practice, the knowledge you have gained will make you a better and more involved member of your directorate, able to participate to the benefit of all. To paraphrase George Orwell, all doctors need to be managers, but some will be more managerial than others.

14 The future

Tim Scott

Predictions

The only certainty we have is that any prediction of the future will be wrong. No matter with what expertise we consider our chosen field, there will always be shifts, abrupt dislocations that are, by their very nature, unpredictable. A recent forecasting experiment asked for predictions of a number of key financial variables over the period 1984 to 1994. The authors of the report kindly, and not surprisingly, anonymized their respondents, since government finance ministers from around the world performed less well than a group of dustmen![1]

One tries to steer a course between Scylla and Charybdis: on the one hand, identifying those broad changes already taking place whose future trend can be judged, which suggest that the future will look very like the present; and, on the other hand, trying to take account of those revolutionary and radical breakthroughs that will totally alter the shape of the world. How many of us in 1980 would have expected to see the Berlin wall come down in November 1989? How many would have expected in 1996 to see the government of a unified Germany once more centred in the Reichstag in Berlin?

Perceptions of change

Our children often give us sharp reminders of changes that take place in our own lifetime. My daughter, now 18, is incredulous to think of a time before T-shirts, yet to any English teenager in the 1950s they were just an American version of a vest. My son does not talk in terms of a career but rather strings together in his mind a succession of interesting projects, each in some way linking to another, and each allowing him to add to his repertoire of skills and become more flexible and multiskilled. Perhaps the generation currently in medical school will worry less about a career then we imagine.

So, in an attempt to avoid these pitfalls, this chapter will not paint a particular future but rather discuss the items in the present that may shape our future. It will attempt to look beyond such questions as the next election and which political party will lead us into the twenty-first century and try to point up those pressures for change that will continue whatever the political environment. Aspects of the changing world, the world of health care and the pressures on the clinical practitioner are set out in Figure 14.1.

Health care issues

The critical health care issue of the early part of the twenty-first century is undoubtedly already with us: demographics. The proportion of the elderly in the population continues to increase, as does the number of people who are over 75 and indeed over 85. As the baby-boomers become pensioners, they are likely to place very considerable additional demands on the health care system. A number of commentators suggest we may see growth in the infectious diseases, not only HIV and hepatitis B, but also possibly new, as yet unfamiliar, organisms. Added to this will be the emergence of a whole variety of health care opportunities stemming from the human genome project and advances in genetics.

Patient empowerment

There is now growing evidence of a global movement that can either be described as patient empowerment, consumerism or even 'paternalism is dead!'

Whichever end of the spectrum we choose, there is no doubt that throughout the developed world we are seeing a change in the nature of the relationship between doctor and patient, between health service professionals and consumers. This change must surely be welcomed and be seen as healthy and positive. If individuals feel more empowered about their treatment, and play a stronger role in co-ordinating and indeed managing their own illnesses, they are then, evidence suggests, likely to have better outcomes. It must surely be a relief as well to clinical professionals if the full burden of the patient's illness is no longer thrust upon their shoulders. Ever since Sheila Kitzinger published her *Good Birth Guide*, the issue of informed choice has been firmly on the agenda in the UK. The Patient's Charter and other aspects of Conservative rhetoric merely reinforce a continuing social phenomenon.

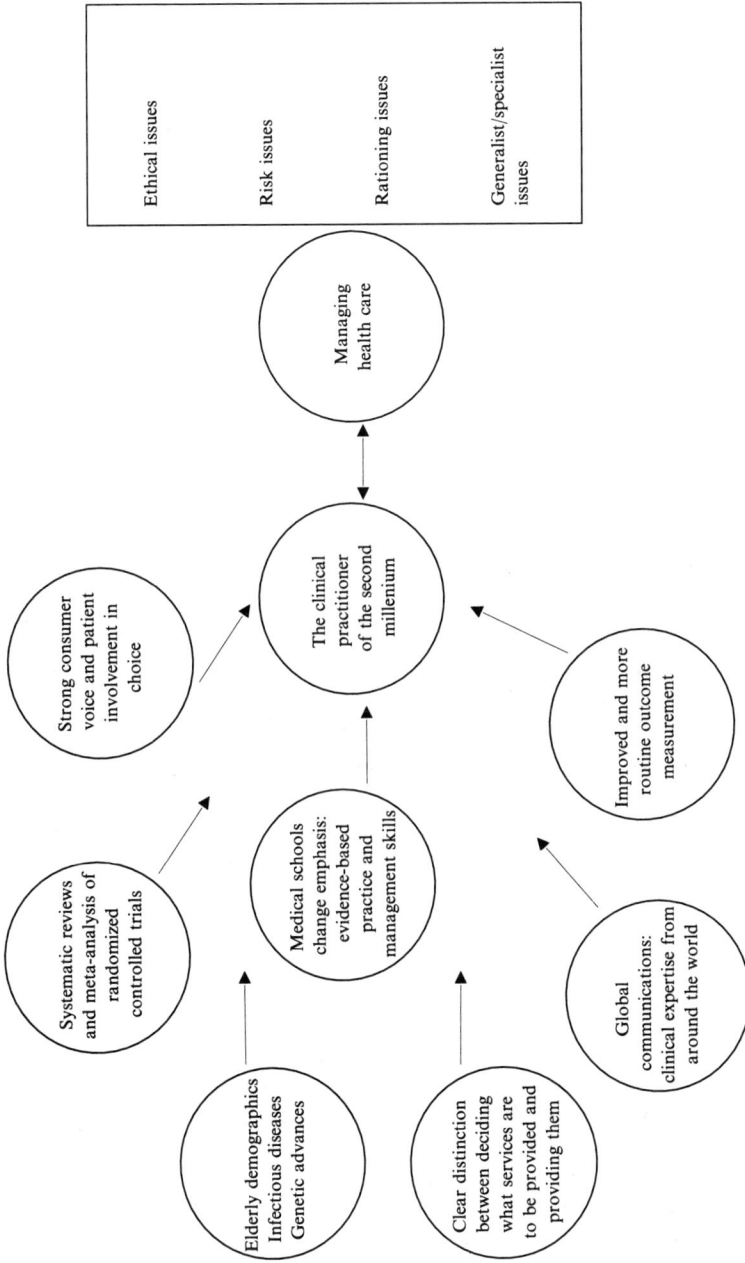

Figure 14.1: The changing influences upon the clinician of the second millenium.

Ethical issues

Risk issues

Rationing issues

Generalist/specialist issues

Managing health care

The clinical practitioner of the second millenium

Strong consumer voice and patient involvement in choice

Systematic reviews and meta-analysis of randomized controlled trials

Elderly demographics
Infectious diseases
Genetic advances

Medical schools change emphasis: evidence-based practice and management skills

Clear distinction between deciding what services are to be provided and providing them

Global communications: clinical expertise from around the world

Improved and more routine outcome measurement

Outcomes

The increasing attention being paid to outcome measurement in health services research, will lead to a shift away from the Holy Grail of a single health outcome measure to a recognition of Maxwell's seven dimensions of outcome[2] and a series of validated tools for routine measurement along a number of these dimensions. As well as this much more regular and routine view of outcome data, there will almost certainly be a shift of emphasis away from the physiological and towards the psychological. This is another aspect of the change in dominance between the clinical professional and the patient; as one patient was heard to mutter recently in outpatients, 'I don't care if my electrolytes balance, I just want to feel better!'

Technology

This shift towards routine measurement of outcome and a review of treatment against outcome is likely to be accelerated and facilitated by the underlying communications technology. It is easy to go along with other social commentators and point to the Internet as a revolutionary change in society; it may well be that, but at minimum it allows for high-speed communication between all parts of the world, and already specialist clinicians are beginning to discuss the outcome of clinical protocols without regard to national or international barriers. The Centre for Evidence Based Medicine in Oxford was one of the first English NHS worldwide web sites (along with Brighton NHS Trust and BAMM) and already supports a lively electronic mail correspondence.

Systematic review

Of course the move towards evidence-based medicine is a total cultural change and paradigm shift. The majority of doctors know in their hearts that they are unable to keep up with current clinical literature, even with a particular narrow and specialist focus. The average consultant, for example, needs to be reading around 30 articles a week to keep up with the published literature in any particular subspecialty. Nevertheless doctors remain anxious to understand developments in their own field and in particular to know of treatments that might improve outcomes for their patients. The emergence of disciplined and expert topic reviews and meta-analysis has been greeted with an almost audible sigh of collective relief by the harassed, overworked, busy clinical professional. Incidentally the new specialism of expert literature reviewer will no doubt develop in its own right, and clinical trials of the future will be even more strongly influenced by the existing trial base.

Specification of health services

The overall environment in which health care is provided from country to country is also subject to inexorable forces of change. Whether we call this contracting, service level agreements or specification of service, there is now a clear contextual divide between the act of providing health care and the act of planning and specifying health care for a given population. As with any paradigm shift, it is difficult to remember how we thought about these things in the past. Recently I was re-reading an NHS case study based on a health authority in the 1970s and was forcibly struck by the total confusion that existed at the topmost levels of the organization, between their role as a major local employer running three hospitals and providing health care and their role as the health authority in determining what health care they should purchase. The battle between the desire to invest in community services and the operational management difficulties of reducing expenditure in the acute sector was never clearly articulated; yet, from the vantage point of the 1990s, it could be much more clearly set out. This contextual framework, of course, offers no new solutions, but it does enable more structured debate and discussion of choice to be made between the participants in that choice.

Rationing and choice

What is unlikely to change in the next 25 years, if ever, is the necessity for choice and indeed for explicit rationing. There will always be a balance to be struck between what we can do and what we can afford to do. Even though we understand, and will understand much more, about the effectiveness of what we can do and the value for money that it represents, as well as the true costs of choices, choices nevertheless will have to be made.

Medical teaching

Information technology, which has to date in health care barely scratched the surface, will, in the twenty-first century, revolutionize medical teaching and training. With the knowledge base doubling every five years, it is becoming increasingly apparent that it is impossible to learn the whole of clinical medicine, and that medical schools will shift from teaching medicine, to teaching how to find out about medicine. One can envisage clinical professionals who are experts at accessing information and whose routine approach to specialist problems is to review the literature and search out the handful of experts world wide. If a patient can be observed in detail by a doctor some thousands of miles away, is there a need for locally available specialists? Far better to have the X-ray scanned by someone who sees literally hundreds of bone cancers than by someone who has seen very few.

Clinical practitioners

There are likely to be major shifts in what we mean by a doctor and by training and development of our doctors. This is increasingly going to be seen in medical schools, where management will not only feature as a core element of the curriculum, covering the use of management techniques in managing clinical practice as well as the management of the organization, but, probably more fundamentally, will also begin directly to impact on what medical students learn. Of course medical students will continue to get a basic grounding and understanding of physiological processes, but the perpetual tension between specialist and generalist roles is likely to be played out in a different way in the future. Some people see specialization within general practice; GPs with 'an interest in', for example. Other specialists already complain that their general skills are so weak that they might be better working in partnership. One is reminded of the story, possibly apocryphal, of a patient lying in a ward at a specialist cancer hospital whose visitor, a qualified nurse, was horrified to find her friend suffering from undiagnosed pneumonia. The ward staff and clinical team were all too busy treating specialist symptoms and looking for aspects of specialist therapies to spot this more general problem. True or not it illustrates the potential dangers of specialization and the need continually to maintain a balance, if not an oscillation, between the two extremes of generalist and specialist care. Generalists will increasingly be taught how to access or promote systematic reviews. The increasing emphasis on research as an extension of the know-ledge base and the need for a continuing process of research aggregation and consolidation will make the whole idea of 'keeping up with the literature' both more important and more straightforward. As well as integrating the traditional narrow specializations, the possibility of contributing simulta-neously to both will be an increasing reality in the fragmented work-load of the twenty-first century.

Ethical issues

The most important knowledge domain for a clinician in the twenty-first century may well be the ethical. Rationing of health care will become more and more explicit as the things we can do increasingly outstrip the things we can afford. Whilst the BMA in their recent publication on 'core values'[3] strongly argue that clinicians must not be faced individually with rationing decisions, there is no doubt that they will be centrally involved in such debates and discussions, although decisions will need to be taken at some kind of democratically elected level of society. The increasingly explicit aspects of rationing will be linked to the wide variety of ethical issues likely to arise from our increasing understanding of genetics and our ability to intervene genetically. If we know that an individual is going to get Alzheimer's disease, do we give them a hip replacement? Being able to advise on the ethical issues underpinning these kinds of decision, as well as helping to take forward and structure the debate, at either the local, regional or national commissioning level, would seem to need special skills, and this may become a significant area of work for some doctors. All doctors, however, are going to want to think carefully about the ethical context of their individual clinical decisions, given the much greater scrutiny such decisions are likely to receive in society in the future.

One clear trend in society is to make clinical decision making more visible and more open to scrutiny. In the USA patients are achieving this through the legal system; perhaps we may find a less expensive route in the UK. Nevertheless whichever route appears, it is clear that the public and patients feel it more critical to challenge and review the decisions of doctors.

Physical environment

What will be the base for the clinical practitioner in the next century? On the one hand we have seen the development of group practices for GPs and the move towards primary health care teams, with a wide range of clinical professionals working in and out of group practice or health centres. In some parts of the country, NHS Trusts are providing consultant support to the larger group practices, and some commentators have suggested the emergence of the polyclinic, already common in some parts of Eastern Europe. As the primary health care centre seems to grow, we have simultaneously seen a change in the hospital sector. Increasingly hospital care is consolidating into a number of major centres, with trauma facilities and substantial intensive care resources, and a network of intermediate hospitals. The DGH network of the 1960s begins to look like gross overprovision. There is also a move to use the fabric more intensively; does it make any sense to use operating theatre suites only during the day time or should we look to 24-hour use of this kind of costly resource? Whatever the balance between primary, secondary and tertiary care centres, it seems clear that practitioners will move more flexibly between them, and that what will be important will be ways of providing points of focus for all practitioners in any area to meet and discuss the ways in which they work together. This may be facilitated by communications technology, but the constant task of linking generalists and specialists is an element of the overall management task.

Health care management in the twenty-first century

It seems that the management of health care in the twenty-first century will have four critical components: the routine addressing of ethical issues, the clear understanding of risk, the need to deal openly with issues of rationing and the management of the generalist/specialist interface. Health care management will require specific strengths and skills in these difficult areas, which are likely to be centrally delivered by clinical practitioners.

Instead of regarding the two worlds of clinical practice and management as somehow different and urging people to 'decide which horse they are riding', or encouraging clinicians to shift full time into management, the only way in which health services can deliver the major task that society requires is for a significant number of individuals simultaneously to practise their clinical skills and engage in the management of the health care system. In parenthesis it is really not such a remarkable thing to ask. In talking about the difficulty of undertaking two different tasks, we perhaps forget the huge number of amateur athletes, many of whom attain county or even national standard, whilst still holding professional jobs. Or the vast number of writers, artists, historians and others, all of whom combine full and demanding careers with unpaid outputs for their creative energy and enthusiasms. If there are difficulties in continuing to practise clinically as well as take significant management roles, we should look to find ways round those difficulties and support and enable those individuals who want to undertake two roles. Practitioners who are engaged day by day in the health care problems of individuals have the credibility and empathy to take on the management tasks of bringing ethical skills, risk management skills and rationing frameworks to bear on the work of other practitioners. They are able to balance the generalists and the specialists. It is critical that the enormous opportunity provided by the NHS reforms is not wasted and that the current clinical directors and medical directors are enabled to provide role models for future generations.

Risk issues

The empowerment of the individual patient, as well as the greater availability of structured literature reviews, places a requirement on clinical practitioners to discuss the nature of risk and the level of risks with individual patients. Informed consent to treatment needs to become a reality, and patients and public are likely to drive hard to achieve this. Practitioners will have to acknowledge their own fallibility in this process; it will not do to assure patients, 'I've done this procedure hundreds of times'. They have a right to know how often it does not work.

Rationing issues

Doctors will inevitably play a part in the discussions on rationing issues, as they have done since it became clear that funds would never be available to do everything that could be done for people. What will become clearer in the twenty-first century is the process by which rationing choices are made. We currently see local decisions in which a locality purchaser, in discussion with stakeholders, makes routine, currently annual, choices of what services to purchase from a fixed sum. As these processes become more overt, it will be important for doctors to make clear their role within them, as participants and parties to decisions, but not as sole arbiters.

Specialist/generalist interface

There will always be clinical specialists and generalists. The task of the clinical manager is constantly to review and monitor the communications between them and to ensure a free flow of information and support. This will be important not only for the care of patients but also in ensuring clinical research is properly linked to the day-to-day world of clinical care.

Conclusions

Looking at the overall picture of the pressures on clinical practitioners, it is clear that they face, as do the rest of us, a turbulent and uncertain future. However what should also be clear is that those people who enter medical schools with a deep and personal commitment to the ill, the poor and the weak in society should find satisfying and challenging roles in clinical management in the next century, where their strong personal values, and the values of their profession, will be critically important to the development of the health care services of their society.

References

1   *The Guardian*. Binmen rubbish mistakes. 3 June 1995.
2   King's Fund Institute (1991) *Outcome Measurement*. King's Fund Institute, London.
3   BMA (1994) *Core Values for the Medical Professional in the 21st century*. BMA Publications, London.

Index

access to hospitals 48
accounting *see* resource management
administrative staff 112
  in directorate team 130, 131
advertising 48
audit
  clinical 15, 81–5, 114
  White paper (1989) reforms 14–15, 81

BAMM (British Association of Medical
  Managers) 12, 140
Baugh, Simon 123
block contracts 58
BMA (British Medical Association) 12, 143
Bradber Report (1954) 7
Brown, Peter 122
budgeting *see* cost aspects; resource
  management
Bunch, Chris 126
business managers 117, 130, 131
business plans 116

Cadbury Report 122
Calman Report 92, 94, 102
capital assets (of NHS) 8
care in the community 28, 33
carers of disabled people 79
CCST (Certificate of Completion of
  Specialist Training) 93
chairman of Trust 110, 116
chief executive of Trust 110, 116
  medical director appointments 121
chronic disease management 63–4
clerical staff 112
  in directorate team 130, 131
clinical audit 14–15, 81–5, 114
clinical coding 51–8
clinical directorates 12, 109–11, 115,
  125–6, 129–31

clinical directors 111, 116, 129–36
  accountability 125, 127
clinical quality management 83–6
clinical trials 81, 87
clinicians *see* doctors; GPs
CME (continuing medical education)
  91–2, 95–6, 101–8
Cochrane Centre (Oxford) 87
coding systems 51–8
commissioning 31–7, 51
  CME and, 107
communications technology 140
community-based care 28, 33
computers 140, 142
consultants *see* doctors
contracts/contracting process 31–3, 51
  contract types 58–9
  contracting out 8
  contracts pricing 15–16, 59–61
  isoresource groups 55–8
  role of clinical director 133
  White paper (1989) reforms 15–16
cost aspects
  cost benefit analysis 20
  price and cost 48, 59
  pricing of contracts 15–16, 59–61
  role of clinical director 133
  see also resource management
CPD (continuing professional
  development) 96, 103–4
CRDC (Central Research &
  Development Committee) 88, 89
Culyer Report 88, 89, 90, 94
customer concept 41–2

demographic aspects 138
DHAs (district health authorities) 10, 11
  FHSAs and 33–4
  priority setting by 20